Sharon,

It was a pleasure meeting you at the 87th BPW birthday. You are very special.

S. H.

Author, Speaker, Coach
www.hinescgl.com
Jan 15, 2009

9/11: PENTAGON S. O.S.
Leadership Strategies of Survival

Trina M. Hines

authorHOUSE®

AuthorHouse™
1663 Liberty Drive, Suite 200
Bloomington, IN 47403
www.authorhouse.com
Phone: 1-800-839-8640

© 2009 Trina M. Hines. All rights reserved.

No part of this book may be reproduced, stored in a retrieval system, or transmitted by any means without the written permission of the author.

First published by AuthorHouse 1/27/2009

ISBN: 978-1-4389-1357-5 (sc)

Printed in the United States of America
Bloomington, Indiana

This book is printed on acid-free paper.

To Workplace Leaders and Employees

And

People Affected by Unexpected Challenging Events

A Special Tribute to 9/11

Remember, Reflect, & Renew @
http://www.pentagonmemorial.net/home.aspx

Contents

Acknowledgements	ix
Foreword	xi
Preface: January 15, 2008	xiii
Introduction	xv
May 2001: An Examination of Self	**1**
Groomed for Advancement	**4**
An Appeal to Duty	**7**
The Locker Room Talk	**9**
Notice of a New Job Opening	**11**
June –July 2001: The Last Scene	**13**
Break the Mold	**17**
Other Duties as Required	**19**
June 2001: Unofficial Arrival at the Pentagon	*20*
July 2001: I Report to Work	*20*
Arrival at the Pentagon: June-July 2001	*21*
Welcome to My New Office	*21*
Responsibility and Challenge	*22*
Tuesday, September 11, 2001	*23*
At the church	*25*
September 11, From a Child's Eyes	*26*
Anthony's Testimony:	*27*
Ring: Your Office is Gone	*29*
Prayer Warrior: Armor of Protection	*31*
I Want the Whole World to Stop	*33*
Friday September 21, 2001: Exhausted but Thriving	**36**
Power Trip	*38*
Hiring Temporary Workers	*40*
Threat Day	*41*
Showdown	*42*
My School Angels: Dr. J	*45*
What Strategies Sustain You through Stress?	*46*
The Day of Decision:	*47*
The Final Act: My Work There Is Done	*48*

Postscript: A Legacy of Pride January 2008   *49*
9/11: Leadership Strategies of Survival (S.O.S)   *50*

S.O.S #1: Strategic Thinker   **55**

S.O.S.#2: Model and Practice   *57*
S.O.S.#3: Seek Mentorship   *58*
S.O.S#5: Know Your Priorities   *69*
S.O.S #6: Role Modeling   *72*
S.O.S 7: Be Diplomatic   *77*
S.O.S #8: Faith Outlook   *79*
S.O.S #9: Make Tough Decision   *83*
S.O.S #10: Lead Effectively   *84*
S.O.S# 11. Flourish with Humility   *87*
S.O.S #11: Identify Ineffective Leadership   *92*
S.O.S #12: Authentic Leadership   *93*
The Ideal: The Leadership Creed   *95*
S.O.S. #13: Maintain Character and Respect   *96*
S.O.S. #14:Clear Communicator   *98*
S.O.S. #15: Lead with Competence   *100*
The Influence on My Leadership Style   *106*
Final Leadership Thoughts: 9/11 Strategies of Survival   *107*

Conclusion: November 2008   **114**

References   **115**

Acknowledgements

There is no way I can thank the multitude of people who deserves acknowledgement for their leadership, teamwork, and kindness who have contributed to this book and my life. To each of you thank you. I express a special appreciation to my husband, Sergeant First Class Anthony Hines (retired US Army) and our three children: Taniesha, Tiandra, and Anthony Jr. To my mother who has supported me throughout my dreams. Thank you to a team of contributors of this book, my military, government civilian, and civilian families that I have gained throughout my military travels. A special thank you to Linda, Command Sergeant Major Terry Robinson, Command Sergeant Major Jose Burgos, Sergeant Pettis, Timothy, Renea, Matrice, Armentha, Jane, Brenda, Diane, Donnell, Tuwana, Johnny Sr. & Jr., Dr. Joan Johnson, PhD, Bishop Eugene Reeves, and thank you God for giving me the strength to survive and overcome the unexpected challenging events in life. If I have forgotten your name on this project, please know that you are appreciated.

Foreword

Retired First Sergeant Trina M. Hines, founder of Customized Global Learning, LLC is nationally respected and well known for her motivational speaking, teaching, and leadership. She specializes in collaborating with businesses, government, churches, schools, and other non-profit organizations helping them to maximize their personal and professional potential. Trina has twenty-five years of cutting-edge leadership experience, speaking to audiences in the United States, Africa, Russia, India, Korea, and Germany. Her professional military career spanned twenty years, during which time she received numerous awards, decorations, and accolades. These include the Legion of Merit, two Meritorious Service Medals, **two US Army Commendations, three Army Achievement Medals, and two National Defense Ribbons. Trina retired from the Army as a First Sergeant in January 2003.** She is also the recipient of the Prince William County Regional Chamber of Commerce Award.

Trina has earned a Bachelor's degree in Social Psychology, a Master's Degree in Education, and is a licensed and ordained minister. Trina has received one Honorary Doctorate in Ministry and is currently pursuing a Doctorate in Education Leadership with Education Technology. As a certified Human Behavior Specialist, she provides training and workshops on Team Management Systems and other high performance assessments for leadership team building, diversity, and stress management.

Professional and personal success lies in understanding yourself and others, realizing the impact of personal behavior. No longer can the influential define leadership just by the roles at the top of the business pyramid, but by the results oriented working relationship between leaders and followers, leaders and peers, and leaders with upper management. This book is designed to offer encouragement, mentoring and coaching to leaders, employees and individuals experiencing challenging situations in the midst of the unexpected. What is the unexpected challenges, I am referring too? 9/11, Katrina, Tsunami… Downsizing, Unemployment, Death, Divorce, Foreclosure. You may have your own list of the unexpected, and that is okay. My goal is to strengthen you at whatever level you are on or encourage you to succeed in whatever situation that you are facing. My primary focus is from the work environment.

Trina is married to retired, Sergeant First Class Anthony Hines. They have three children.

To learn more about Ms. Hines and Customized Global Learning, LLC visit: //www.sos.pentagon.com or http://www.hinescgl.com.

Preface: January 15, 2008

Something is special about this year that makes me feel I need to complete this book as soon as possible. The number seven signifies completion and this will mark the seventh year since the September 11 attacks on the World Trade Center in New York City and the Pentagon in Washington, D.C. The number eight stands for "new beginnings."

In July 2007, I started thinking it was time to write about my experience as a survivor of the attack on the Pentagon on September 11, 2001. As a novice writer, I did not know where to start. What I did know was that I wanted this story to be an encouragement to the reader. With so much going on in the world, I felt it was time to do my part to help someone to move forward in his or her life when faced with life's challenges. I have changed the names and locations in the book, except for the Pentagon. The military and civilian rank status and positions mostly removed. This was a difficult decision since I am military and have a great deal of pride for the military. The final decision to remove most of the military titles and position is for easy reading.

While writing this book, in no way did I try to measure my experience or level of personal pain with others. Although we may want to identify with others' pain, as we naturally should to bring encouragement, this is often a difficult, if not an impossible task, since we are not walking in their shoes. The one thing I do know is that joy, pain, suffering, and grief will come across our paths somewhere in our lives, often when least expected, but we must find the strength, courage, endurance, and discipline to continue after a crisis arises.

Why discipline? Because discipline is doing what needs to be accomplished, regardless of how you feel, while having the endurance and integrity to perform the task when no one is watching. In life, you face the unexpected. There is no perfect scenario when this occurs.

Know you are doing your best and move forward. If you fail or feel like circumstances are challenging you to fail, you can find the inner strength to get up, clean up, and move forward. You are a survivor destined to help yourself and others to overcome the very thing and issue that was meant to stop you. Your negative will become your positive. Just watch and see!

Introduction

In this book, I want to address strategies of survival primarily at work and within leadership in the midst of challenges. Challenging situations may be thrust upon us by unexpected events; such as personal challenges, economic, financial, natural disasters, or even terrorism. Yet, true leadership stands the test in the midst of great challenges, as was discovered through the events of September 11, 2001, Katrina, and other unexpected events. I want to address qualities of effective leadership from an experiential life application, which includes principles of stress management.

If you want to build the organizational structure for the future and build revenue in an organization, you must take care of the people who work in it, both while the organization is financially profitable and when the unforeseen arises. It is amazing to me how many times I hear leaders say that taking care of people is their number one principle, but if you ask employees of that same company what is one of their greatest concerns, the answer you are more likely to receive is, "Leadership does not understand how to relate to us." This is a critical factor of workplace stress in an organization. We must ask ourselves has leadership forgotten what it felt like to be an employee? On the other hand, is the situation that employees do not understand the pressures faced by leaders?

Effective leaders are those who have not forgotten what it entails to be a follower in some capacity or another. These leaders know how to build people, capacity, and revenue for the organization and get assignments completed while taking care of the people in the process. An effective leader is one who has a basic understanding of behavioral preferences, since behavior is observable, and personality development as revealed by that behavior. Understanding is furthered gained through observation, training, and assessment. An assessment does not define a person, it just brings awareness that people are unique and that, under certain situations or in particular environments, we operate in a given manner. Effective supervisors are able to identify when people on their team are operating outside of their normal characteristics when under stress and now demonstrate signs and symptoms of a need for stress management. These leaders also have an accountability partner, someone who can help them identify when they themselves are operating out of their norm.

Further, effective leaders are those who respect and celebrate cultural differences. One of the most relevant things I learned living in an overseas country for a short time in the military, was when someone called Americans foreigners. "Oh yes," this is what I said to myself: "Trina, you are a foreigner. Although this host country has welcomed us to provide them with military support, you are a foreigner, so it is your place to learn from their culture, respect their culture, and not force your culture on them." Similarly, effective leaders understand organizations are a blend of races, genders, cultures, and talents. This is what makes us unique. There is much to learn from cultural diversity, particularly for any company wishing to be successful in today's global marketplace.

Although this book has some theoretical approaches detailing an effective leadership model and stress management techniques, the first part of this book really serves as a diary from the heart of one leader to another, from an employee to another employee. You are reading the actual notes from my personal journal From May 2001 through January 2003, and to keep the integrity of the journal there are a few parts that may repeat a particular portion. Further, this book will encourage, uplift, and inspire. One reader may hear the voice of my heart; another leader may hear points for a case study, while still another reader will hear the challenges faced by a working wife or a mother.

In this book, you will find brief implied reference to the question of whether women should be in the military, or in leadership positions anywhere, and some of the stresses faced by women in the workplace. This is to help leaders to look at diversity from a gender perspective. Recently I had a woman tell me she felt sorry for me, since I was working in an organization designed solely for men. I responded to her, "Could you imagine corporations, businesses, or governments without hearing the voice of the woman?" Women bring a unique perspective to any organization and equal knowledge, skills, and abilities not having women management, leadership, or an active team player is a disservice. Respectfully, no offense to men intended, ninety percent of my mentors while I served in the military were men.

May 2001: An Examination of Self

I found myself engaged in self-evaluation in May 2001. At the time, I had been in the military for many years and was quite comfortable in my position. Nevertheless, my family's needs for stability and continuity began to appear more of a concern to me than any need for further career advancement. Changes were coming, and I had a decision to make. The unofficial word was that Company B, in which I was working, was going to through "realignment" in the latest Army realignment, a nice word for downsizing or elimination. Since I was nearing retirement, I had to ask myself, "Is it time for me to stay in the military and try to make the highest senior military enlisted rank or should I retire?" This is a question of reenlistment was not a new question, as I discussed this question with my husband who was also a military soldier at each time of reenlistment. Reenlistment is volunteering to serve more years in the military, after you have served the subsequent enlistment. In order to prepare for the next promotion, I would have to go to a military school for about nine months and move to another location after school. I really love my family and the decision I make affects my family. Our three children were getting older and having a permanent place to call home was important. I really liked my military job, which allowed me to make leadership and managerial decisions for military personnel. The military was good to our family; allowing us to travel abroad, provided quality education, housing, child care facilities, and I could add to the list; however, this is not a sales pitch. Yes, there is the risk of losing my life for my country, but I did not see this as any other risk of possible life in any other part of society.

A good leader is a strategic thinker, evaluating herself and her decision making process. I needed more information. Therefore, I asked my eldest daughter, who had recently turned fourteen, about moving. She was very emphatic when she told me that she did not want to move any more. "Well," I thought within myself, "Does she really understand what it takes to financially raise a family these days?" I realized right away, what a self-serving thought this was. Her opinion matters. Furthermore, when I considered how she moved from state-to-state and overseas eight times by age eleven, I could not readily imagine moving her again. Good leaders operate under the Platinum Rule: "Treat others as they want to be treated" (Alessandra, 2008). This rule has to include my family, or it is worthless. I need to consult my family.

When I asked my husband about moving and going to school, he said, "It is up to me." However, he really seemed to like his military job. "Now what do I do?" The last half our military career he was selected for a prestigious job supporting the government. Who would want to give this job up? His military career is exciting, challenging and rewarding which is not to say that it was not before, and I can tell that he really likes this job.

Now who should make the sacrifice or compromise? Either, I will move to a new place, which means he would have to give up his job and we would have to live separate "locations" for an unknown amount of time or may be this is a sign to finish this goal. We were dual military, the proper term for word for separate location is "an unaccompanied tour," the politically correct wording when you are separated from your family due to a military commitment. I thought to myself, "Be careful Trina," goals are not worth at the expense of your family. You have enough time to finish this goal and do something else. If you stay-in you may obtain more awards, but what will it be worth if it is at the expense of your spouse or children?" Now, here is my opportunity to make a crucial sacrifice, which is giving up what I enjoy for the overall good of my family stability.

Considering the needs of other parties involved and the effect of a decision on their lives is a trait of good leadership. I feel the Platinum Rule again in the pit of my stomach "Treat others as they want to be treated." I asked my youngest daughter, who was nine, and my son, who was four, about moving. Moving did not matter to the youngest children.

Once I knew where my family stood, it was time to examine which options would accommodate their needs while enabling me to continue my military service. I would have to find a balancing point between their needs and my aspirations or get out of the military altogether. I dreaded mentioning thoughts of leaving to my senior military supervisor, especially since he has been grooming me for the next promotion for quite some time. I thought to myself, "What am I going to do now?"

Groomed for Advancement

I remember traveling to a senior military forum out of town. Every year in Kansas (remember locations are changed) senior military leaders get together and have the opportunity to see the new military equipment associated with their jobs. They also have the opportunity to network with other senior military leaders. No junior military leaders received invitation to this leadership event, so there was the opportunity to be yourself among your peers.

My military supervisor must have figured I was not a genius in this area, because I lost track of how many lectures he gave me prior to going to this forum. When I arrived in Kansas, I had my own rental car, so I drove to the hotel. It was not the hotel where most of the senior military leaders were staying, but across the street. I wondered, "What kind of treatment is this? The last time I checked, I was a senior leader, too. He is my supervisor, not my father." I could have chosen to be offended, except somehow I knew that what I did not know, or see, probably would be in my best interest. I now realize that he was exercising another trait of good leadership: structuring a situation so that the employee makes the right choices.

While at the event this supervisor introduced me to leaders who had been on some of the previous promotion boards for senior leaders. In the military, in order to obtain a promotion your records receive a review by a military board. The people on the military board are selected senior leaders handpicked by other officials in the military. Once a year they review everyone's record to determine if you are ready to receive the promotion to the next senior military grade. You do not know whether the same people in Kansas will review the records because the selection process is secret. However, after the announcement is made of upcoming selectees for promotion, rumors of who had been on the board inevitably follow. If you ask these leaders directly they will never tell you, but through the process of elimination, you have an idea, because they disappeared during the time for the selection board and their whereabouts was somewhat cloudy.

The leaders I met spent a lot of time explaining how the next promotion would work with regard to what type of future jobs to seek. I began to dread even more having this upcoming conversation with my supervisor about leaving the military.

The Talk

A few months passed and I finally worked up my courage and went to my supervisor's office, intending to bring up the subject with him. As I was going over some reports about military personnel, I casually slipped in that I was thinking about getting out of the military. He looked at me and chuckled. He did not seem to believe me, so I told him again. He asked me, "Why do you want to do that?"

I told him, "I just think it's time. I only have eighteen months before I will be eligible to retire, and I do not think I want to continue."

He replied, "If you are not sure, you will probably regret it later."

"Yeah," I was thinking,"but was it worth the possibility of losing my family in the process? Where do you draw the line?" Keeping a professional look on my face, I said, "It's just that this next promotion is going to be hard on the family. We will have to move again, and I moved around a whole lot in the beginning of my career." I know moving a lot and family separation is a natural part of the military life, but now at 18 years in the military somehow something seems different.

At the time, it did not seem as if my supervisor had heard what I was telling him, as he went back to discussing the reports. I would soon find that not only had he heard the true motivation behind my desire to end my career, he was working behind the scenes to eliminate the reasons for my separation.

An Appeal to Duty

Today, my senior military supervisor asked to meet with me in the conference room. This is a normal request; when we have a lot of material to review, the conference room provides adequate space to hang charts and look through documents. When I walked into the room, he had a fellow military supervisor, a highly respected leader from the event in Kansas, there with him. This man was quite a transformational and charismatic leader whose accolades spoke for his high military rank. As I took my seat, I wondered what the nature of this meeting would be.

The two of them told me, "You know, you have a good opportunity to make the next military promotion. There are not a lot of minority females in senior leadership positions in this career field; you are a good role model and have taken the right job assignments." This was a clever approach. A good leader knows when to appeal to pride in a job well done. Such a leader will remind an employee, whose commitment to the company is wavering, of an obligation to mentor their fellow employees. This appeal plays on my sense of duty, not something easily shrugged away. These two supervisors continued to speak to me, providing a very logical case for remaining in the military: "This company will probably close soon, which means the soldiers in it will be sent to other locations, whether you take your next promotion or not. Are you sure you want to retire?"

Here they had me, since one of the reasons I felt a need to separate from the military was the fact that my family would have to move. What difference would it make, knowing I would have to leave this company regardless? Faced with the fact that a move would take place either way, the balance began to tilt toward staying, at least for the moment. Wow, in my think and think process, I did not have an answer. A good leader will structure a situation so that the employee makes the choice that best meets the needs of both the individual and of the company.

"Honestly, I really do not know," I answered. Here I sat a person who liked critical thinking, problem solving, and decision making, with no answer for myself!

My supervisor leaned forward and said, "This is what we will try to do. We will see if there are any job openings in this area. While we do that, you will have more time to make a decision. No promises, "he stated." "Since you are in a senior selected position in this company with a time in position requirement, completing your time in this local community area could work in your favor."

Now the balance was tilting even further toward the company. This supervisor had taken an objection designed to take me out of the company and turned it into a reason to stay. I left the meeting thankful, yet still unsure if I was going to stay in the military.

The Locker Room Talk

Several days after talking with the two supervisors, I briefly talked to the female leader who shared responsibility for the entire military post where I had been serving at the base near Lorton, Virginia. I did not know her personally prior to this conversation, but her picture was posted at various locations on the entire military installation, so she is really important. I recognized her when I saw her in the locker room. Now to me personally, she was a role model. High rank, articulate, professional appearance, professional dress: hair always neatly pulled back, starched uniform, and highly shined boots. I heard nothing but great things about her. You could tell by her demeanor that her outward appearance was just a reflection of her character.

Since she was in the locker room pinning up her hair and did not look occupied, I decide to ask her my question. "Excuse me," I asked, "may I take a moment of your time?"

"Yes."

I am wrestling with a decision to stay in the military to prepare for a new journey, or prepare to get out of the military. "How do you know when it is time to retire from the military?"

"That is a good question." She turned from the mirror, looked directly at me, and said, "My husband, who has just put in his military retirement paperwork, told me, 'You will know. You will wake up and find that it is just not FUN ANYMORE.'"

Now, I must admit I wake up many days and think, "This is not fun." It is especially not fun when the phone rings in the middle of the night. No one from the military calls you at home in the middle of the night with good news. When the phone rings, you wonder who is in jail, who has had a fight, or you hold your breath and hope it is not about the death of a soldier's family member or about a soldier in your command. Yet, there is such a sense of pride when you know the decisions you make daily affect not only employees and the company, but also, ultimately, the future direction of the world. Additionally, whenever you have a soldier compete and win a championship, get an award, perform a heroic act or just finally get something "right" that they kept getting "wrong," there is a sense of pride. Knowing that the job you do allows Americans to sleep peacefully fills your heart with a sense of duty. The long hours and the sacrifices to keep others from having to pay the ultimate sacrifice is a part of the call to duty. However, is that the definition of fun? Somehow, there must be a different definition of fun. I set the idea aside for the moment.

NOTICE OF A NEW JOB OPENING

I soon found there was a position open in the Pentagon similar to the job that I was currently doing. My job description consisted of taking care of people and of making sure that we, as a company, accomplished the tasks and jobs assigned to our company. These tasks included keeping morale high, maintaining discipline, assuring completion of necessary training, and ensuring the physical health and welfare of the soldiers under my supervision.

Organizations have their cultures, sets of beliefs, values, formal and informal norms that they follow within their organizations. The Pentagon is no exception with one distinguishing mark that was difficult to describe, "Political." I could never define politics until my retirement. I knew that the politics existed; I could feel the effects of the politics, but there seemed to be no concrete definition for it. The day I retired, I realized that politics is not based on a definition, but on an experience. It is how you manage to work through bureaucracy successfully while maintaining your integrity, dedication to duty, moral ethics and accomplish the task at-hand. Any political situation requires the use of diplomacy.

Diplomacy is the practice of giving respect and deference when and where it is due while remaining steadfast about carrying out your given duties. It demands that paths be clear, communications enhanced, and bridges built. Diplomacy is not a zero sum game, with one winner and one loser. It does not mean unconditional surrender to the will of others. Diplomacy means knowing when to push and when to soft pedal. Nothing is accomplished by going head-to-head that will not leave an injury somewhere in the organization. Diplomacy is the better option.

Part of my military training had taught me how to assess a situation prior to getting involved within the organization. I knew that I would have to do some fact finding first: to whom would I be reporting? Which personnel would it be my responsibility to oversee? How would I locate them in order to bring them into compliance with the directives I had been given? Locating soldiers sounded simple from a military perspective, but this was the Pentagon and somehow many of the soldiers had blended into the civilian culture. I needed to know what types of communication styles worked best with each person. What leadership style would be most effective in motivating everyone to embrace the necessary changes accompanying my tenure? Further, evaluating the training needs, assessing their readiness, fitness levels, and help them brainstorm the most effective methods to achieve their personal and organizational goals and responsibilities were a part of my responsibilities.

I knew that I would not be able to simply go in and throw my weight around. This is inexperience leadership to go into an organization making changes without proper assessments. I would have to coordinate the military training schedule with each directive respective work schedule, minimizing any impact on their ability to continue to perform their civilian duties. I would have to build trust, both with the personnel for whom I was responsible, as well as with the directors of the various departments in which they worked.

Building trust is a challenge, which every leader in a new position of authority must face. Key factors that lead to the establishment of trust are consistency and respect, as well as making the effort to get to know the organizational needs to be met, and the wants, needs and goals of the individual employees for whom I would be responsible. It is vital to learn as much as possible about the motivations of personnel if you wish to have any level of success in leadership. I must admit I thrive on new challenges, so I think I am ready for my new adventure. Is this a sign that things are working out in my favor to stay in the military and meet the needs of my family concerns?

June–July 2001: The Last Scene

When a film director has finished shooting the last scene of a movie, the director says, "That's a wrap." This is how I am feeling as the end of another assignment approaches. I reflect on the past, present and new future that lies ahead. I think on the good, bad, and indifferent situations experienced, always reminding myself of the importance of seeing the positive in the midst of challenging situations. Now who will replace me in this present organization? The date of the organization closure has not been set and I need to move forward to the Pentagon assignment. Actually, I have given some thought to my replacement since the conference talk. Today, it is time to have a Talk with Leadership.

Leadership replacements for nominated positions or senior leadership selected positions usually come from outside of the organization, so when I put my two cents in regarding who should be my replacement, it was met with silence. Silence is not necessarily bad. It means the senior leadership will think on it. I have earned respect through my hard work, setting the example, and self-discipline. My words will not fall to the ground empty.

The person I recommended had supported me and our organization the entire time I was in the leadership position at this company. Anything I needed, he ensured that his soldiers were always present to accomplish. He also trained the soldiers well, leading them by example. He never hesitated to speak his mind while looking out for the interest of all involved. Every leader wants to have someone like this on their team. Someone you can trust.

"Amazing," I reflected, "less than a year ago he and his wife and I experienced the worst crisis of their lives." Well, they experienced it. Because I had learned the importance of being a support for soldiers in crisis, our organization was there to uplift him and his family in an untimely situation. It was a day of grief that I will never forget.

I had gone about my normal routine of the day: physical exercise with the soldiers at 6:30 am, taken a shower, grabbed a cup of coffee and then had gone on to work. I was concerned about this senior sergeant because he had not shown up for physical training that morning. That was quite uncharacteristic of him. Something just did not seem right. No one had heard from him.

I spend very little time in my office, so before I left for meetings and checking on resources and personnel, I pulled out my phone roster and called his house.

The sound of anguish was heavy in his voice as he answered the phone, crying.

"What's wrong?" I exclaimed. My heart was now beating fast, but my voice remained calm.

"COME NOW, COME NOW! My baby died last night. She was only six months and she's DEAD."

My mind was racing, but I had to think on my feet. "Where are you? Where are you?"

Strangely, I had the phone roster, so I knew his physical address. It just came out of my mouth. Somehow, when an employee is in trouble, my entire mindset, changes and moves to crisis intervention.

Hearing his wife sobbing in the background, I tell him, "I am on my way! Hold on!" I rushed out the door and got into my vehicle.

9/11: Pentagon S.O.S.

"Think Trina, Think." Somehow I maneuvered my way to his house, but the trip is still a blur, because I am sure I did not go by myself. Very seldom as a female leader, do I travel to a crisis situation alone. I know that I ran to the door, opened it up, and went into the house. In the dark, both he and his wife were crying and sobbing. Their pre-teen son was sitting in a chair, just staring at them.

En route to his location, I had already called the hospital for a chaplain to come to his house. A house call by a hospital chaplain was out of the norm. Normally, you have to bring the person to the hospital, but at that time I did not care about the norm or what would be acceptable, I just needed some help. A good leader is willing to take a calculated risk to defy the norm, in order to save someone else.

Their precious baby, who had been sick at the daycare the other day, had died in her sleep. The soldier had kept the wife's pregnancy a secret; they had tried for twelve years to have a child; and now, the six-month-old baby was not here. There are times as a supervisor when you do not have the answer or the right words. All you can do is be a support system and help your employee move forward at a rational or reasonable pace.

I must admit, I have a high respect for our organization and the military support provided throughout the post during this time of crisis. Compassionate teamwork is critical in times of sorrow. The organization coordinated housing, so this soldier could bring his family from out of town to the funeral (home going). The entire company pitched in and provided food and financial support. This soldier platoon provided communication to one of the prestigious military organizations and they volunteered to provide the funeral service.

I stood in the cemetery after the funeral service. There are days when you just do not understand. "WHY?" These are the days you go home and assess "what really matters."

It is hard to believe that this happened a little over a year ago. I observed this leader move forward in the midst of a great personal challenge, and maintain his professionalism. This was my recommendation for my replacement: a genuine, compassionate leader, who would understand how to transition soldiers when the company dissolved.

Break the Mold

Specialist Jane Doe called to inform me where I was going to be working in the Pentagon, but I had already received written notice. Specialist Jane Doe was a single soldier, soon to be a new mother. She was pregnant and wanted to talk to me about her concerns. I found that a little unusual for her to be so upfront, since I was not working at the new location, but that is just part of the job. There are certain expectations of a senior leader and one of those is listening. Therefore, I listened attentively. She was not sure what to do with regard to staying in the military, but she liked her job. How would she manage with a new baby as a single mother in the military?

This is something most working mothers face at some time. Working mothers everywhere have to balance their desire to be with their children and the demands of their career. This is a demand today that affects fathers as well, but I still think the decision is a little different for men. In the military females face an additional challenge, because military deployment can take one or both parents away. Military women know the rules, there are the few who welcome the opportunity to serve in military deployment or combat apart from their children. Other military women will roll the dice and hope their number does not come up. Still others understand it is just my job.

All married dual military (husband and wife) and single parents serving in the military sign a contract that says, "If you deploy or need to be away from your family for any extended time you must have someone to care for your children." Of course, someone might think that we are gambling with our children, but that is not the case at all. Both groups are patriotic in serving their country, preparing for combat, and protecting the interests of the nation. Times are changing, and the unpredictable makes you have to make the best decision for your family based on your present knowledge.

My own self-analysis and my assessment of my situation served as preparation for advising this female soldier, who felt she could talk to me. I quickly assessed the situation and decided not to try to work with the entire military service issue now, but to deal with the situation at hand. This promoted the leadership questioning side of myself.

I asked her, "Do you have any family here in the DC area?"

"No." she responded.

"Who will go with you to the hospital when you have the baby?"

"I will go alone," she responded.

"I will go with you if you want me there."

"That would be great," she responded.

She went on to tell me that a Caesarean section was prearranged, which allowed me to schedule this very important appointment. "Well," I think to myself, "perhaps my work in the military is not yet done. Preparing soldiers for the possibility of war and fulfilling the mission of the military is an expected part of leadership responsibility. Yet, the personal interaction with soldiers in need makes me question if I have fulfilled my responsibility. I am glad I have a little time to accompany her before it is time to move forward with my career or retire." What a preliminary experience prior to the official arrival at the Pentagon! I wonder what else is in store?

I kept in contact with this soldier after that conversation, and I met with her once or twice. Then off we went to the hospital. I went in with her when she had the Caesarean section. I just could not imagine her going in alone. The very nature of my job gave me a sense of obligation to provide support for my fellow employees. What an experience!

Other Duties as Required

The doctors gave me a seat located at her head. There was a blue sheet that was between her belly and neck, so she could not see, nor could I. I slid to the side with my chair some so I could see what was happening. One of the nurses asked if I was going to be okay, because some people faint during cesareans. I said, "Yes."

"So that is how a Caesarian section works? It almost doesn't look real." A neat cut went across the stomach. I remember when they brought the baby out of her womb it looked like baby powder was all over the baby. I thought, "Hey that's not what is in the movies. " Okay, Trina, you might need a little more exposure in this area. "It's a boy," the doctor has spoken. Oh, how wonderful. Here lies the future of a new generation. The baby, covered in white powder, breaks the mold and marks the future of a new generation.

Exhausted and leaving the hospital, I think this is absolutely, amazing. I guess I am still having fun: being able to support a fellow soldier in such a personal way. I cannot help feeling a renewed sense of purpose when I witnessed the birth of this child. I realized then the importance of support and mentoring, not only for the one receiving the support, but also for the one giving it. Support and mentoring can counteract stress and improve employee retention when you are able to get outside the office/military mindset and take part in "real" life to revive your sense of purpose. This is a great job. I wonder how this would translate on a resume.

June 2001: Unofficial Arrival at the Pentagon

When I arrived at the Pentagon to meet my new supervisor, he was not very cordial. His conversation was short, to the point, and he acted as if I was interrupting his time. This unexpected attitude and cold reception reminded me of my early days in the military, when I had learned that there were leaders who did not live up to the standards set by the Army Values, core values that people should govern their behavior through leadership and respect. However, I had learned not to let anyone else's attitude or actions stop me from doing what I knew to be the right thing or control my attitude. I did not clearly understand why he was so dismissive, but I had a job to do, and I would remain optimistic in doing my job.

Full of anticipation and ready to take on my new responsibilities, I asked my supervisor where I would be working and his reply was, "I do not know." He would probably find a cubicle for me somewhere. I knew then this assignment was not going to be an easy task. Any time a person tells a military leader responsible for taking care of several hundred soldiers to work from a cubicle, something is wrong. How will I maintain confidentiality on soldier privacy issues from a cubicle? I thought, "Does he not understand the responsibility of a military leader?" Later I would find out that I was wrong. This was the Pentagon. Most military leaders were fortunate to get a chair, desk, and cubicle. Working from an enclosed office would be a miracle!

July 2001: I Report to Work

It was hard to say goodbye to the soldiers from my previous organization, but I was content that Mark's selection as the interim replacement was the right choice. I remember getting off the elevator with some reluctance, since apparently my presence was not particularly wanted. It put me in an uncomfortable position, but I had confidence that I would be able to work through it. Reality is that people go to work daily where their presence may or may not seem welcome. A good leader does not whine about the situation, but finds opportunity to change the atmosphere. As I walked into his office, I watched his countenance. I was quite certain I observed, again, his perplexed look. He looked up and said I was moving to another organization, which was in the upper management of the organization and that I would have more influence, and then he nonchalantly mumbled something about change. I said my farewell and with the new instructions in-hand I headed for my new job, leaving his office with a sigh of relief.

Arrival at the Pentagon: June-July 2001

Many people probably viewed pictures of the Pentagon or the actual building itself. Anyone who has ever visited the Pentagon will attest to the fact that the Pentagon is similar to the size of a small city. Walking from one side of the building to the other side of the building is similar to maneuvering through a maze with the hope of making it to one's destination without encountering a roadblock or getting lost. Leave early, wear comfortable shoes and carry a cell phone becomes part of the daily ritual. It is not as if the cell phone will work inside the Pentagon, but if you manage to maneuver to the center of the Pentagon, you will find an outdoor courtyard, where you can make a phone call and cut your walking time in half.

Welcome to My New Office

Located in the new, renovated side of the Pentagon are Sam and John. I learned that I would have two supervisors, but answer indirectly to six supervisors when and if necessary. Sam, John, two senior executives, colonel, and a military officer outside of the Pentagon. Sam was a calm and somewhat laid-back person who senior military had just arrived at the Pentagon. John was a charismatic senior civilian manager, with a distinguished professional demeanor. Wow! What a welcome relief! I liked their attitudes. John explained I would get his office in the new area of the Pentagon (1E470). He was moving to a special wing in the Pentagon.

The meeting and greeting had gone very well. However, Sam and I still needed to know what our responsibilities were going to be. Apparently, the key civilian leadership felt that the soldiers in their organization needed closer military training, mentoring, accountability, and preparation for when they departed to their next assignment upon leaving the Pentagon. Consequently, when they found out Sam and I were coming to the

Pentagon, they diverted our assignment and nominated us to two military positions. They then proceeded with the selection process and chose Sam and me to carry out the task. I wondered how they knew so much about my background, but again, it is the Pentagon. I began to wonder if there was anything they could not accomplish or find out. , I was in my office and beginning my new journey.

Responsibility and Challenge

Yes, I have acquired a challenging position. Sam and I are to locate all soldiers in this organization of three thousand plus employees, set up a military training plan and conduct physical training with them. Next, we would set up an administrative personnel tracking system so that senior executives could have access to this information and be aware of any given employee's military status at all times. Apparently, some of these soldiers were getting lost in the shuffle, losing out on promotion opportunities as a result of not keeping up with their physical training and ongoing military education. Many of these individuals wound up separating from the military; this resulted in a loss of investment in their training, as well as the loss of their experience and input in training future soldiers. Our challenge was to produce solutions to prevent costly loss.

One particularly interesting challenge we faced was that the soldiers worked in fifteen different directorates, or departments, which means that there were fifteen directors who were responsible for ensuring that these soldiers performed their duties at the Pentagon while remaining mission-ready. We would need to enlist the cooperation of each of these directors. Previous experience with change and transition had shown me that people often resist change. I was not senior to the other directors, so from my position, the changes we needed to implement required that I collaborate with the right networks and understand that some will still resist change. According to my understanding and equally as challenging, most soldiers working at the Pentagon had become a part of the civilian culture. They wore civilian clothes and intermingled into the civilian organizational formal and informal norms. I thought, "How would we be able to find them?"

Sam and I had decided that the most efficient way to find everyone was to stand outside the cafeteria for several days in a row, dressed in our uniforms. We would then learn which employees were military by their greetings to us. This idea was a great success, and we soon identified our personnel and were able to implement the tracking program.

The remaining challenge was that corrective actions, duty rosters, and possible punishments for infractions or dereliction of duty delegated to a chief officer who worked outside the Pentagon, now required sharing of the responsibility with Sam, myself, and our staff. I would personally have to work through him and his advisor to identify these men and women.

I had just begun to lay the groundwork for this task when it seemed as if the whole world blew up in my face.

Tuesday, September 11, 2001

On September 11, I was working in the Pentagon on an ordinary day. There were not any signs or symptoms that this would be an unusual day. Having completed physical training with the soldiers, I showered and headed to the office. At the office, I checked the calendar and found a notice on the schedule to meet with several soldiers in my office that morning.

A few minutes after 9:00 a.m. there were two soldiers waiting outside my office to speak with me. One required personal and professional counseling and the other was the soldier's supervisor. I normally operate on a fifteen-minute rule, meaning if a person is fifteen minutes late without a previous notification, cancel the appointment. The supervisor and soldier showed up about 9:15 a.m. and apologized. I conferred with the soldier briefly and decided to reschedule the meeting for Wednesday, since Sam had just called simultaneously with an important message.

Sam told me I had to be in a different meeting elsewhere in five minutes. This meeting that Sam and I had to attend was to help us to understand how the organization functioned.

Normally, I do not cancel a meeting to attend another meeting, but the soldiers had arrived late and it was important for Sam and I to build relationships with key leaders in the organization that was new to us. It was about 9:25 a.m. in the morning when I left the office and swiftly went to the designated room for the meeting. I was moving through the corridors of the Pentagon at a fast pace and hurried up three flights of stairs. Arriving at the designated meeting area, I realized I had left the point-of-contact for the meeting and Sam was not there at the location. I asked the receptionist if there was an Army meeting there and he responded that no Army meeting in this Air Force location. I called an executive manager and asked him to look at the schedule. He began to talk about the Twin Towers of the World Trade Center in New York and to say there probably would not be a meeting, because key people were probably watching the televisions inside the Pentagon. I did not get the relationship of what he was saying. Plane hit Twin Towers, it made no logical sense to me. I thought I misunderstood what he was saying, so I asked him if he could give me the room number again and check the schedule. As he began to check the schedule, he said he did not see a meeting.

About that time something hit the Pentagon. It violently shook the Pentagon. I ran out in the hallway, and people were running. It was controlled chaos. I asked what was going on, and someone responded that it was a bomb. Someone responded, also, that the Pentagon had been hit and to get out of there fast.

Quickly, I hit my pants pocket and realized I had my car keys and cell phone, but not my wallet. For a second, I thought to go back and get it, along with my checkbook, but because everyone was running out, my gut feeling was that it would be wise for me to just get out. My office was empty with no personnel in there, so there was no need to go back. When I got outside, some people were staring at the Pentagon, as if in shock. I was looking at the Pentagon and I did not see any physical damage. The security guard was yelling "GET OUT, GET OUT!". Another plane was coming in and expected to hit right away. Everybody had to leave.

Because I had left my wallet behind in my office, I knew there was no way I would be able to get on the military post. I decided to drive to my local church and leave a message there that I was okay. My husband was out of town and I knew if he could not get me, he would check there. His scheduled flight had him leaving Kentucky at 6:00 in the morning and flying into the Washington, DC area. When I got to the church, I used the phone and called my mother. At the time, I had discovered that the cell phones were not working because I had tried to call her, my supervisor, and military leaders. Cell phone networks extremely swamped with calls, people trying to find out anything they could about loved ones, and emergency service personnel using them as well, trying to stay in communication. I knew if I did not contact my mother, she would call the White House. Very briefly, I spoke to my mother and told her I was okay.

At the church

Early on this day, my day started as a routine day, but certainly it was no longer a routine day. When I arrive at the church, all I can remember at the church was the church administrator, Patricia Sport.

I was curious about the church events of that day, so I asked Patricia Sport the administrator of the church and the Senior Pastor Victor Reeds about what they recall about this day. The events you are about to read about was written in 2008.

According to Patricia Sport, "I got to the church about fifteen minutes after the first plane hit the first tower at the World Trade Center and minutes after the second plane hit the other tower. I remember Pastor, Reverend Butler, Lisa, and myself being there. We had set up a television setup in the fellowship hall and while we were doing that, someone told us that a plane had hit the Pentagon. Pastor led us in prayer in his office, and received phone calls began to come into the church. Calls from members who had families in the Pentagon and they were asking for prayer. I remember Pastor Hines' sister calling to ask if we had heard from you (Trina). A deliveryman arrived with a desk we had ordered and just broke down crying in the hallway. You came in soon after that and later we received a call from Pastor Hines letting us know that he was okay as well.

Bishop Victor Reed Thoughts: The morning of September 11, 2001 started as most Tuesday mornings for me. I met Pastor Jim Green for prayer and breakfast. We were eating and he got a call from his wife and said that the World Trade Center was on fire on TV. Therefore, we finished eating and hurried to the church on Cable Road to see what was going on. We actually watch the second plane hit the second tower and we knew we were under attack. We then started to receive calls from people in the Pentagon and were told that it had been hit as well. We all stop work and began to pray for the situation in our country. We do not know what was happening we just knew that something very evil was going on and many lives were being lost. We began to pray for the safety of the people that were trapped in the burning buildings and that the people we knew in the Light (our church) that was working in all of the government building.

We then tried to call the ones were knew on the cell phones but all of the circuits were busy and we stop and prayed some more. One of my employees Reverend Morgan began to weep uncontrollably because he had relatives that worked in the buildings, he was from New York. We tried to comfort him but to no avail we just called his wife and had him picked up and sent home. We continue to pray by this time the phones were ringing off the hooks and all the members were calling asking about different members that worked in the Pentagon and asking what could we do, and I told them all to pray. Later we learned that all of the folks were safe from our congregation and we let out a sigh of relief and gave God praise.

September 11, From a Child's Eyes

Part of my responsibility as a military leader was to know the addresses, phone number, and locations for over four hundred and fifty soldiers assigned to the 15 directorates within the Pentagon. Every break in the phone line, I could find, I started calling supervisors' cell numbers to find their whereabouts, and soldiers with no contingency plan in place at the time, this situation caught everyone off guard. While all these events were taking place, my children were still at school. I still did not understand the United States was under attack. I left the church and remembered that I had an extra accountability roster at home. I was on the phone getting accountability of soldiers, the day I could see a 911 through the eyes of our eldest child. Our eldest daughter was thirteen, our youngest daughter was eight, and our son was four. I did not realize the anxiety that my eldest daughter felt from, not knowing what had happened to me. Here is her voice, as I asked her to write about how she felt that day.

My eldest daughter came home from school that day visibly shaken. When she walked into the house, I was on the phone getting an accounting of the whereabouts of those soldiers who worked in the Pentagon. I hung up for a moment and she said, "Mom, why didn't you pick me up from school?"

I asked her "Were you worried? I am sorry, I felt you were safe. I didn't think about the fact that you might be worried about me."

She replied "Mom, the plane went through the Pentagon."

I told her she should not be afraid or worried as there were angels over her and angels over me. "You'll never go before your time." I did not want her to be overly concerned about the events. Then I got back on the phone. Later, I had the same talk with my second daughter and son, who were not aware of the events of the day.

Our eldest daughter's facial expression continued to remind me that she was upset, and that many of the parents had come to the school and taken their children home from school. Through her eyes, I could see that she had been worried whether both of her parents were safe. I really just did not want her consumed with fear, so I explained to her that angels watch over you, and she really had no reason to fear. I thought it was the right thing to say at the time. Well, I will conclude that her eyes spoke that I did not win the Mother's Day award on that day. If I could turn back time, I would have picked you up. I am sorry dear.

Anthony's Testimony:

Anthony, my husband perspective of September 11. Anthony had been in Kentucky and possibly scheduled to be on the plane that went down in Pennsylvania. He changed his flight information due to his soldiers' request the night before. When he got off the plane, he went to the Pentagon and just stared in shock, not knowing what had happened to me. A big part of the emotional damage that day was to the number of people who were waiting in dread, not knowing who had been killed and who had survived. There was a feeling of shock that something so horrific could even be possible. This was the United States of America, the strongest nation in the world. Something like this could not possibly have happened. I wanted to hear from Anthony more about September 11, so I asked for more details, dear.

Anthony Thoughts: Anthony, said, "This is an account from Jim a team member who resides in the Washington, DC area." On or about 5:00 am, my team, Jim, and I arrived at the airport in Pittsburgh, PA. Upon checking in at the ticket counter, one of the team members observed that two Middle Eastern men looked as if they were attempting to board the planes with two long knives. The airline receptionist would not let them on the plane, so they asked to talk with a manager. Our flight was scheduled to depart in a few minutes so we gave no more attention to this matter.

After departing Pittsburgh, the team arrived at Reagan National Airport at approximately 7:45am and we caught a cab, which passed the Pentagon on its way to Anacostia, D.C. While putting their bags in the car the same team member noticed that plane was off its regular flight pattern and voiced it to the rest of the team standing there. Everyone continued to load their bags into their cars, not realizing the events that were transpiring.

A few minutes later we saw smoke from our company's parking lot, coming from the northwest part of the city. Next, I got into my car and headed home toward Virginia. While passing the Pentagon, I noticed that it was smoking. Trina worked in the Pentagon and was at work at that time. I stopped on the side of the road and walked to a group of people who were standing and watching and inquired of them what had happened. One of the people standing around said that a plane had flown into the Pentagon. I did not believe them, so I walked toward another group of people and asked them what they saw. They repeated the same thing as the other bystander.

Then they asked me if I had heard what happened to the twin towers in New York. I told them that I had not heard anything. They then informed me of all the events that had transpired. I tried to contact Trina in the Pentagon, but all lines were busy. I tried to call my job agency, but all lines were busy there as well. There was no way to communicate at that time. All communication systems were fully saturated.

After things had settled down a little, details of the 9-11 events became clearer. The flight that gone through the Pentagon and the Pittsburg flight perhaps intended to fly into the White House, were both planned to make a profound statement to the United States. The terrorists wanted us to begin to fear and become paranoid and begin to mistrust each other, and the leadership of this great nation. Instead, it brought more unity, dignity, and pride.

September 11 is a reminder, United States, to let us know that freedom is not free .

Ring: Your Office is Gone

It was mid-morning when I received a call. The person on the other end said, "Are you okay?"

I said, "Yes, I am okay why?" It was Sergeant First Class Jones. He and Colonel Smith had maneuvered into my office area, looking for me. They thought I might not have known how to get out of the building because I was still relatively new to the Pentagon. He informed me that my office was gone; people burned, charred in place. He had thought that I was dead as well. I told him that I had been trying to locate him and six or seven in our organization who were not accounted for.

I do not remember how I managed to speak with supervisor Sam, but I do know that I met him at the Pentagon, shortly after the call. I had no military identification with me, but prayed for a miracle. I just needed to be there. Luckily, no one asked for any military identification, the guards let me use my Pentagon badge to get into the Pentagon. I did not have time to worry if that was right or wrong. Usual or unusual, the plane had hit the Pentagon and had created chaos and my prayer for access granted sufficed for now. I gained entry into the Pentagon.

Walking though the Pentagon that day was so eerie. The building lit by emergency lighting seemed echoing quiet. Supervisor Sam and I walked through to see who or what we could find. We went to the fifth floor, the main floor where our headquarters office was located. This is where some of the key official offices resided, such as the Secretary of the Army and the Administrative Assistant to the Secretary of the Army. Everything seemed so cold, dark, and spooky. We did not see anyone, but you could smell smoke and some other odd smell. We went down the stairs. It was very dark until we reached the basement. As we began to walk through the basement, we saw a light and actually walked into a military operation center. I was glad to see them, and they were glad to see us. Not everyone from that center had evacuated the building. They also informed us that there were soldiers up on the top floor working. I do not remember the exact time this was, but it was still early morning.

We walked to the top floor and found it filled with smoke, but we still were able to find the place. The soldiers and the civilians were surprised to see us, and we were thrilled to see one another. They asked for protective masks or some type of surgical mask to help them with the smoke inhalation. Sam and I assured them that this situation was priority, and we took care of the situation right away. Sam and I were not able to get to ground zero; we had to leave to go to an offsite location concerning the events. Initially, it was hard to believe my office, 1E470, was twenty feet within the collapse area so that it is correct for me to say that it was ground zero. There were 40 people in our organization that died of the 184 within the Pentagon (including American Airlines Flight 77). If I had not gone to that meeting in the wrong room that actually never existed on that day, I could have been 185. If I had stayed in my office with the two soldiers, the number would have been 187. Even if I had returned to my office when the Pentagon was hit by the plane the fumes and the fire from the plane could have taken me out permanently. There must be a purpose for my life that has not been fulfilled, yet.

So many innocent lives taken by the unexpected. My heartfelt prayers go out to the families, friends, colleagues, and concerned parties. We cannot change the events that occurred and it is even arrogant to think that we can change some people's negative perspective about 9/11. Someone asked me within the last several months whether I thought 9/11 Pentagon was a conspiracy? I chose not to engage in the conversation with the person. However, I did ask them how the events had affected them personally. My concern for this person asking me this question was whether they had found healing, hope, and strategies to assist them in overcoming? The person did not respond. Let us look at some more heartfelt thoughts about the events during and shortly after 9/11. You can hear how one's faith (or lack of) can affect their situation. Later, in the book you will hear a more theoretical perspective of survival strategies.

Prayer Warrior: Armor of Protection

In the military, we wear body armor when there is a possibility that we might sustain injuries. The body armor does not guarantee full protection, but it reduces the impact of injury or loss. When I think about the events of September 11, I think about all of the amazing people who worked tirelessly during the events. When you begin to name them and you leave one out , someone might be offended. Therefore, I want you to know_____(fill in your name or organization) that you are not forgotten and still appreciated. There is one group of people that I want to take time out to talk about briefly and that is the millions of people who prayed for divine intervention. If it were not for Prayer Warrior, where would we all be? A prayer warrior is a combatant soldier willing to join in a fight and stick with the fight until the battle is called off.

In the two weeks prior to September 11, 2001, a Prayer Warrior who has since become my friend was at home for the first time in twenty-five years of ministry. All of the staff at her local church were laid-off due to downsizing. She tells that she was now waiting on God for a new assignment or orders on the direction to pursue. I know her to be a woman of prayer, and I asked her if she would share if she recalled anything unique about the day of September 11th.

Hannah told me that back then she had felt uneasiness and had felt burdened and restless about an unknown concern. As the week of 9/11 approached, she had called relatives and friends to check on them, thinking that perhaps one of them might have had something for which God was calling her to stand in the gap. Her inquiries turned up zero answers. All seemed normal and well with each of them.

By the Sunday evening before the infamous Tuesday, my friend had begun pacing around in her home like a caged tiger. Finally, in exasperation, she cried out in prayer stating that she must have the comfort of Scripture. My friend told her husband that she was going to pray. With her Bible in hand, she told me, she cried out to God to reveal the burden to her and His direction for prayer. My friend says that she heard Him say: "Look at Second Corinthians, chapter ten, verses three through five."

"3 For though we walk in the flesh, we do not war after the flesh:

4 For the weapons of our warfare are not carnal, but mighty through God to the pulling down of strongholds;

5 Casting down imaginations, and every high thing that exalteth itself against the knowledge of God, and bringing into captivity every thought to the obedience of Christ;" (KJV)

Her next question was: "God, what stronghold are you talking about?" Was it a personal or family, regional or national stronghold? She says that she waited and finally drifted off to sleep. The next morning my friend awoke to her husband's early rising for his work as a schoolteacher. Again, she reached for her Bible, hoping that there would be further revelation on what she had heard from God the previous night. As my friend told her husband good-bye, she says she felt tired and weary and decided to lie back down for a little while. By now, it was between seven and seven thirty in the morning. No sooner had my friend laid

9/11: Pentagon S.O.S.

her head back on the pillow, than in one single bound she was standing erect beside her bed and praying loudly.

Hannah walked into her living room, hit the stereo, and repeatedly played the beginning of an inspirational CD. Then, she told me, a travailing weeping cry came over her as she cried aloud to God to tear the stronghold down, wherever it was. This went on, she said, until the phone rang and she heard her husband's voice on the other end telling her to turn on the television, for there had been a great tragedy in New York City. While he was still on the phone, their son-in-law from Dallas called for the same reason. Her husband ended the conversation to return to his duties. My friend and her son-in-law prayed fervently; as they, together, began to go to strategic war in prayer for this situation. My friend told me that she believed, at that point, that a worldwide prayer went into effect, as fellow Americans and the world awakened and heard the news. Only God knows for sure what further tragedy was averted that day when the sound of His people weeping ascended to Him and remorseful prayer was made all over the nation for deliverance from such evil. Our hearts go out to the families, friends, colleagues, and concerned people adversely affected by these events, and we pray that their pain has lessened, since that day. The memories will never disappear from some lives. Hold on to the positive memories, when negative circumstances encourage otherwise.

I Want the Whole World to Stop

While my supervisor was off meeting with some of the senior leaders in the Pentagon, I was visiting with the soldiers. One of the many soldiers was under extreme stress from the job. I received a call from the soldier's supervisor to connect with this soldier. Yes, almost everyone was actually experiencing stress. There was no way at the time to measure the level of stress from this event. Contacting the Pentagon chaplain, together we went to check on this solider. It was a day I will never forget. I can hear the words of this soldier ringing in my ears. The soldier said to me, "I want the whole world to stop, I want the whole world to stop and go find my friend, who is somewhere lying over there in the rubble, while we keep working." I paused because deep down I wanted the whole world to stop too, but I understood the Pentagon was the heart of communication and that would not be feasible. I looked at her and said, "So do I, but if we stop what we are doing, we would let the terrorists get the best of us."

I used that line in a motivational speech I wrote about a year ago. I thought I would add it here. I flew to Colorado to get some assistance in writing the speech and capture the speech on video. I knew I wanted to be a help to someone going through a stressful situation and add to the encouragement the person may or may not receive since the events of September 11, 2001. Further, I heard the National Speakers Association was recording demos, and I did not want to prolong working on the speech any longer. I wanted to capture the essence of this experience and do a reminder to continue to bring more light to this dark day. Here are excerpts from the speech:

"I want the whole world to stop too, but if it does, then we will let our personal terrorists get the best of us. How many of us face our own personal terrorists on a day-to-day basis? We are driving down the highway, minding our own business and someone comes and drives up on our bumper. They are honking their horn. We move over and they drive along side of us and give us gestures not worthy of repeating. Sometimes they even jump in front of you: Highway Terrorist.

How about school bullies? Our children are faced with an alarming number of school bullies: before school, after school, on the bus and on the Internet (Social Networks). I remember when I was young, I was very thin. I used to wear these long dresses and long socks. I used to put rubber bands on the top of the socks and fold them over the rubber band. I remember I was on the school bus and the rubber band was showing. These girls in the back of the bus started to taunt and tease me. I had to make a decision. Would I let these girls get the best of me, or what? I chose to ignore them and tell someone of importance. Bully Terrorist.

What about the bully in the workplace? So focused on getting the job done, getting results, this person forgets that they are really only as strong as the people who support them. This terrorist pretends to be your ally, while belittling you at meetings, thinking you are not smart enough to find out. Workplace Bully.

What about do death do you part from the marriage vow? You gave 10 good years to this marriage only to be surprised by the spouse who says, " I want a divorce" I do not love you anymore. You sacrificed personally for their dreams to come true and when they finally made it to the executive level, CEO status, or highest position in office they said, "You made me do this." Mental abuse terrorist.

Five Motivational Resolve(FMR): Principles to Live By

Life and its situations have taught me and coached me to implement some very important principles.

FMR1: If people do not add value to your life, ignore them. Meaning, do not let their negativity take root in your heart.

FMR2: "Keep your friends close and your enemy closer." In fact, do not let them know you know the difference.

FMR3: Failure is an option. Choose to try, anyway.

FMR4: Fear is not an option. So just do it.

FMR5: Forgive often while thinking optimistic thoughts.

We can choose to do something positive with our experiences. We have all we need within us to affect others. You survived, now as an over comer, help someone else overcome. I am communicating to you to choose not to allow the terrorists to get the best of you. You have a particular audience in life to reach and through what you have experienced in life, and overcome successfully, you can now reach out to others to help them achieve their goals, dreams, and their purpose.

Friday September 21, 2001: Exhausted but Thriving

Today I am so tired. Top leadership is so busy and stressed and rightfully so. I must admit, I am stressed too. The death toll keeps rising; it looks like we still have at least thirty five to forty people not accounted for. No one has time to give themselves assistance, me assistance, and wow, I am tired. I feel like I could use somebody to talk to. Leaders are not immune to doubts and fears, but the expectation to carry on despite their limitation is there, whether real or perceived. The "...suck it up and drive on..." mentality is not effective over the long term, though. Leaders who ignore their own signs of stress and exhaustion will eventually wear themselves and their staff members out. Supervisors need to identify stressors of their leaders when leaders cannot or are not willing to identify their stressors. Someone needs to "check" the "checkers", for leaders will wear a mask for concern of what others might think, not realizing that they are just human beings who are not immune to challenges.

I remember the air filled with intense fear after the September 11th attacks. It seemed like every sound or alarm that went off created panic for some people. I remember being at work when practice alarms sounded to test for emergency. I noticed several of my soldiers would panic: just freeze in place. One time an alarm went off at the Pentagon and I had to physically assist one of the soldiers frozen in place. In this case, you know your limitation for others and get them some counseling and this is what the soldier was referred to. It was tough, and I must admit I could feel the tension, too, but it was important to try to remain focused, because as a leader we needed to be strong for the soldiers. My stressor was not the alarm, my stressor was finding the right help in a stressed and stretched out situation. Yet inside, I could hear a little voice say, "You seem to be handling this well; are you okay; or are you wearing a mask?" Let me go check myself out.

Sam was in an unusually quiet mode and was taking a very long time in making decisions. I guess that is a good thing, since I like to get things done. You have to have balance, especially since so much is going on. What I did not completely understand at the time was that his approach was healthier than mine in the long run. In a crisis such as the September 11 tragedies, shock affects decision-making. Taking time to reflect before acting meant that he was able to remain calm and collected, something that stressed or traumatized workers needed to see in order to keep their own fears from becoming overwhelming. Still, I did not want to burden him, so I decided that I would go visit the chaplain.

Stopping to see the chaplain in an attempt to clear my head, I quickly discovered that he was stressed out . Poor chaplain, Overworked," he murmured" I realized he is only one person, but at the same time, I thought he needed to be mindful not to murmur too loudly. Helping is his job. He might need real prayer if he presents himself in a manner that looks like the leadership of our organization is not supporting him. It is strange how critical we can be of those we believe are there to support us. However, just as I was wondering about his attitude, someone for whom I was responsible might be wondering about mine. It is better to give people a measure of grace, you might need some one day. I decided to talk to supervisor Sam about getting the chaplain some help. At first, he did not take to the idea well, and I perceived it implied that the chaplain should get his support from God only. I had to remind Sam that if God wanted to do all the work, then he would have never created doctors, therapists, social workers, and lawyers. I wonder when we say, "God, please help me," does He think "Why not check the Yellow Pages."

Power Trip

Sometimes those who are located nearest us can cause us grief. There was one military leader who was a major pain, or rather a cause of stress, who attempted to affect our organization. You always have one who swims upstream while everyone else is going with the current. The "bunker mentality" is another sign of poor reaction to stress. Instead of reaching out to work together, people who go into "bunker mode", become islands in themselves, convinced that their immediate needs are the most important, and that protecting their power base overrides the duty to help others. All of the leaders within our organization were working well together. This was not the time to think about "territory" or protecting domain; it was about doing what was necessary to get the job done. Still, this leader further reminds me of how you will have one member of your family that is unusual or unique in their qualities. You know, like Uncle at the family reunion or Auntie at Thanksgiving. Sometimes the things they do are humorous, and then sometimes they can be a little out of control, yet they are still your family. Whether this family member is the life or death of the party does not really matter, as long as they find a way to get the attention or control. Power trippers. Power trippers create resentment within the organization and create a lack of trust. I am proud to be a part of an organization that recognizes when key leaders have stepped over their boundaries and will not allow their behavior to destroy the morale of their organization. If I was to say that all of the leaders in our organization got a long well prior to 9/11, I would be misguiding you. Amazing tragedies make many people put their personal feelings aside to look at how to make things better for the organization and the people within the organization. What if we worked daily from that bond of unity and thought about how many workers will work to build revenue within their organization instead of just fulfilling their job description. As the leadership within the Pentagon of my organization was working well together, a military leader who had some administrative responsibility over the soldiers within our organization was causing additional challenges. One of the reasons that Sam and I were nominated for the position in our organization was that the executive leadership wanted the administrative , personnel, and training duties of soldiers to be guided by military leadership within the Pentagon.

9/11: Pentagon S.O.S.

The military leader who works outside of the Pentagon keeps calling my office looking for soldiers to handle minute details. At first, I was wondering why he was calling me, when I work for senior managers and a higher level of management where this call is more appropriate to task soldiers. I returned his call out of respect thinking he just made a mistake. Borderline harassment is how his conversation went toward me, but this is not the time for me to get my senior leadership involved. I have to count the cost and think how to handle this situation appropriately. I was thinking I cannot wait until the reorganization strips him of some of his power. "Okay, Trina, wrong attitude you have to look at this from the right perspective." A natural part of any work environment is understanding you will work with difficult people, but never left a difficult person bring you down to their level and act inappropriately. Based on the documents on file, this military leader has been way over the line with his scope of authority for some time now. Are you looking at the cause or an effect? "Think, Trina, Think."

Perhaps this why he is trying to cause me grief: I am a new leader and he has no checks and balances in place to ensure fairness. I told myself, it was not me personally by whom he is threatened, it was the new position that represented change. Organizations will cease to exist eventually if they are not willing to change. The workforce today is multicultural, multi-ethnic, and a blend of generations working in a rapidly changing global society. Leaders affected by change will use their power base to support or hinder change. Leaders who fear losing power may resort to coercive power based on fear, intimidation, and punishment to maintain control. The signs and indicators can be overt or subvert. Good leadership is never asleep; they have their eyes and ears open to distractions within their organization.

I remember talking to Sam about this situation with this leader just in case the situation tried to get out of control. It is wise to seek counsel before making decisions that can have an adverse affect on the organization, your employees, or you. Sam told me that you have to remember that change is a process and that I cannot stoop to his level and start kicking and screaming to fight a wrong with a wrong to make things happen. The Pentagon can be political and I could get hurt in the process. Oh, how I remember this lecture, as he gave this lecture with another senior civilian director present with whom he had consulted. I told myself, "Okay, Trina, keep your cool, confirmation of what you were thinking, don't stoop to his level. If leadership did not think you would know how to handle yourself within this environment, they would not have selected you to handle the job. Yet, I wonder what Sam meant by "kicking and screaming." Do I sound emotional? Okay, I do not have time to focus on this now, so think Trina, think.

Hiring Temporary Workers

At a meeting not long after the disaster to discuss personnel needs, one of the directors said, "I just cannot bring myself to do it." He was referring to hiring temps. The senior executive said, "I know it is tough, but we have to bring in temporary workers to do the missing people's jobs."

"Wow," I thought to myself, "this fills me with mixed feelings because I understand both executive's points of view, but I do not like this situation." I remember just talking to Jane in my office about a week before September 11. She was the only civilian still in our office reception area. We briefly talked about her taking a trip to Africa. When I left my office on September 11, no one was in there. I wasn't expecting her to come in the office, as she was preparing to move to another location in the Pentagon. She died that tragic day and now we have to bring somebody else in to do her job, too. The word "replacement" is not the right word to use, because you cannot replace a person who has died or is missing in this manner. Hiring a Temporary to Permanent employee seems more appropriate. At the same time, as the senior executive, you know that someone has to get the job done. The sooner they can get temporary workers in place, the faster we can begin to rebuild. As tough as making a decision such as this is, leadership must know when it's time to get replacements.

Then I tried to think how it would feel to be the Temp. I could only imagine how it would feel to be one of the temporary workers coming into this situation. It would take a lot of courage to intentionally go into a field where such horrific loss of life had taken place, for no logical reason anyone could understand. We would also have to ensure that the people who had survived the tragedy could grieve about their lost coworkers without failing at their jobs. They needed an outlet for the stress of not knowing if, or when, another such tragedy might strike. Being on high alert for so long could shred the mildest temper and weaken the thoughts of the toughest soldier, never mind the civilians, many of whom were parents of young children, retirees, or singles with little support systems. Yet, there was such a patriotic pride, which I felt because leadership was doing a fantastic job and the Temps would work with great patriotism.

Threat Day

When shock wears off, another stage of grief is anger. Did I speak this into existence or what? I am angry; downright mad. This is so uncharacteristic of me. Remember Trina, do not let anger linger, very seldom does it lead to positive results. Yet, I cannot deny how I feel today and just when I thought I had managed through this aspect of grief, something else happens. I get a call from a soldier telling me this same military leader, the one who works outside the Pentagon, has called him personally and threatened him about having one of our soldiers do a certain detail (duty). Now I just had this roster automated in my new office, which is another story, and had put all the information required into the system, and there is no way we have scheduled someone for detail. I guess he figured he would go directly to the leaders who work for me. The soldier is upset on the phone and I tell him, "Do not worry about it, I will handle the situation and take responsibility."

This is a situation could get out of hand, so I briefed Sam about the situation. I knew that if I make a decision while I was annoyed, I would probably regret it later. I also knew the limits of my authority in the situation and needed to make sure I did not operate outside of the military guidelines. I am thinking this leader will try to use legitimate power, a legal power to see, if he can maneuver me into making the wrong move. Yet, I know that the 450+ soldiers and key leadership expect me to represent them well. As I was talking to supervisor Sam, I knew what he was going to say, before he said it. Sometimes you just want a confirmation.

"Do not worry about it Trina, his scope of authority is going to change, pace yourself." I remember thinking that war was imminent, soldiers and civilians were starting to panic and expressing that they could not come to work. However, in the military it is different. A civilian can call in sick and not go to work. You cannot do that in the military. You have to go to the doctors and get a note that says "You are sick and you need to stay home." I am proud of anyone, civilian and soldier alike: who comes to work in the midst of this situation. "God give me the strength to carry the load I am supposed to carry. You have equipped me, so that means this day is a day of peace and not confusion. Will I get fired today?" I guess, we will have to just wait and see.

Showdown

Sometimes you have to stand your ground, even if you have to risk removal or reassignment. I received a message that I needed to go see the supervisor of this same troublesome military leader. "At this point," I told myself, "I really do not care if I get fired." Well, I did care, but I would not bow down to rallying accusation or subtle threats. Somebody needed to get this military leader under control. Sam accompanied me for a showdown.

I am not much of a western show watcher, but I think something happens at sundown. Two people come together face to face to see who will draw their gun to shoot the other first. I was not surprised how the showdown ended. Doing what is right is not always popular, but as a leader, I have learned to follow my gut instinct. Never bow down to an organization bully.

I was sitting in front of a military leader who was giving me a lecture about military protocol, respect, rank, and so on. Sam came along with me, because I was going before one of the big people on the military post. I was informed that this military leader had written letters to have me removed and my rank taken away. Now the process is not that simple; it would take a military court martial to facilitate this process. I knew regardless of what this military leader, now acting irate, could write up would not be based on facts, but his perspective. Perhaps he was use to getting away with such behavior, if he was able to get his overall mission accomplished.

There is a place where you go in your mind when it really doesn't matter. I was not angry, or scared. I just knew that deep down inside I was doing the right thing and accomplishing what the senior executives asked me to accomplish when I arrived there. Now it's a showdown. Do they really have my back? If I have made the right decisions, right moves, then yes, they will have my back. However, having my back doesn't mean I have the right to run to them when I am in trouble. If I need to run to them every time I am in trouble, perhaps I am not a leader. This was my test to determine if I would have a passing grade.

I was waiting for my accuser to show up; however, he did not. Before I was going to see the one with the big guns, his deputy continued to give me a lecture. Once this deputy finished stating what he could have done to me, I politely explained to the deputy why this military leader was way out of control and that his adviser should have gotten him in control a long time ago, because this is just not the way it is supposed to be, Sir, with all due respect. I was quiet for the rest of the meeting, well, kind of quiet.

Sam summarized his perspective by one sentence, "She is doing what I told her to do." That was the end of the discussion. I had to go back into my thinking mode when I was taught throughout my years in leadership that as a woman it does not look good to be emotional. It was not my leadership style to play the "woman card", but I was mad. I pressed my lips together, giving a small smile, and together, Sam and I went back to the Pentagon.

Before I could get back to work, I was called to see the colonel and John separately. The colonel said, "This same military leader has sent emails to us personally about you, don't worry about it. You are doing a good job."

I go to see the supervisor, John, and he asked, "How was your day?"

I told him that it had been somewhat tough, but I made it through. I did not tell him what I had just experienced. It didn't matter because he said, "I heard you had a bad day, and we are aware what is going on. You are doing a good job. Move forward." Well, their confirmations let me know that not only did they have my back, so did the senior executives. Their eyes and ears are never really closed.

When I came home my husband could see how exhausted I was and he said, "I just couldn't imagine if I had come home from work on September 11 and had to explain to the children that you did not make it in the Pentagon." Somehow, the rallying accusations seemed so minute again.

I am still here to have a bad day. Somehow, the day doesn't look so bad after all. I wish I could tell you that the military leader outside the Pentagon antics stopped, but he didn't. The next thing I remember was that I had to report to another leader in the Pentagon who worked outside of the organization that I worked for.

This time I gather my statistical data, charts, and analysis of the work accomplished for the organization and the soldiers assigned. With a 4-inch binder of work related information, I met this leader in the outside center of the Pentagon.

"Trina, I keep hearing about a female who is in the Pentagon just kicking up dust and I just wanted to meet you personally." I was taken back for a moment, because I was not expecting this kind of greeting. He said, "You remind me of myself, when I arrived at the Pentagon. I knew I was doing the right thing in the midst of change, but was met with much resistance. Just when I thought about giving it up, I turned around and looked at how many people were following my leadership." I just wanted to pass this along to you. Remember just when you are about to give up, turn around." He left.

I learned to do my job, and do it well, through the midst of adversity. We will all have a personal enemy. No, not all of them will go away. There may be some enemies, we have to endure while we move forward.

A classic quote says" Keep your friends close and your enemy closer." – Sun –tzu , Chinese general & military strategist (~400 BC)

Later, I added, "And do not let them know you really know the difference."

What happened to this leader? Nothing. What happened to his advisor? He was fired. I mean moved to another location that suited his leadership style. In addition, I moved forward to complete the job I was originally assigned to accomplish.

My School Angels: Dr. J

I had been attending graduate school online during the time leading up to September 11. I remember sending Dr. J an email expressing to her that I was not going to be able to get my homework in on time. The plane had taken it away. No, not the dog ate it, the plane had destroyed it. During this time, Dr. J. just encouraged me to take some downtime for myself. "Go away and pamper yourself. Just do something for you."

Well, I did, and I did it well. Eventually, I went off to the Ritz-Carlton hotel for a weekend alone. I ordered room service, shopped in the attached mall, and visited the spa. I started making this a quarterly routine, to go away and unwind during this process.

My husband asked me with a smile one day, "Honey, can you try to find a cheaper way to manage stress?" At least I think it was with a smile. Kind of look like the smile I had in the office after showdown.

There were other ways that I learn to managed stress. I would take a nice hot bubble bath with candles. I listened to soft music with no words.

I watched comedies, avoided negative speaking people, confided with one friend, and asked her to watch me, just in case I started acting out of my character. There are other methods that have been proven to be effective, such as breathing slowly. Slow breathing never worked well for me; I could never get my brain to slow down fast enough. You can give yourself more time to make decisions. Reduce caffeine. Simplify tasks. Exercise. Live one day at a time.

What Strategies Sustain You through Stress?

One of the main methods that helped me through tough situations is Prayer. Prayer is defined as two-way communication with God. I prayed a lot; although I think I did most of the talking, I think I had so much to get off my mind then. Well, I must admit, I have gotten better on the listening side. I started learning to get rid of things that really did not matter. I also learned the value of just saying "No". "No, I do not want to do this," or "I am sorry I do not have the time to accomplish that." I found that some friends and family members where sensitive to the situation and somewhere not.

There are many excellent stress management techniques that are on the market; you have to find the ones that work for you. If it is not working, do not be ashamed to get professional counseling. Finding the right professional counselor is similar to shopping for a doctor. If you have a broken leg and you do not like your doctor, you won't say, Forget it. I will let this leg heal on its own." Or at least, I hope you will not try this. You will look for another doctor. Do the same for yourself, if needed. My friends, if you know someone who is dealing with a stress related issue or Post-traumatic stress assume that they will readily seek help. You might have to be their advocate, coach, or friend to encourage them to seek help or assist them with the help.

My personal faith in God continues to sustain me. I have a favorite part in the Bible that says in Psalm 91, "He that dwells in the secret place of the most High shall abide under the shadow of the Almighty. I will say of the Lord, He is my refuge...thou will not be afraid by the terror (emphasis added) by night, nor the arrow that flieth by day ...(vs1-5)."

I would speak to myself, "I am not afraid. I will not accept fear, because I am hidden by God." This doesn't mean that those who lost their lives on that day were not hidden. There is evil in this world and as long as there is evil, people will do bad things. No one knows when it is going to be their time to leave this earth. The only thing for certain is that we will leave.

On that day, I had been challenged. My faith was challenged, as the name of my God was associated with permitting terrorism. The God that I know did not tell people to kill others in the name of God. Our founding fathers built this nation under God. One nation under God… It hard for me to believe that we all do not believe or have faith in someone or something. Even those who say they do not believe in God believe in something. Whatever you believe should build hope and encouragement. My heart goes out to all the families who have been affected by this event. May you be strengthened daily to find peace, if you have not found it yet, and be able to move forward with your life.

The Day of Decision:

All the work had now been done; we had successfully gotten all of the soldiers back into uniform. They were getting their necessary training and time had now been set aside once a week for them to focus specifically on military related topics and training. It was not one hundred percent participation, but the numbers were growing. We were working together with the troublesome military leader to get details accomplished satisfactorily. His power was relatively under control; though occasionally he would blow up, for the most part we were able to get the job accomplished. The entire personnel department had been rebuilt. It looked like the rebuilding of the Pentagon was on schedule, and it would reopen on time. "Now what do I do? I guess it's about that time now. It is time to submit my retirement paperwork. It's not fun anymore."

When I speak of fun, I do not refer to a state of temporary excitement. Fun is that rush that you receive when moving from beginning to end. It is the sense of accomplishment that is felt when a difficult task has been completed. I had that gut feeling that this is the positive note; I wanted to complete my successful career.

When the plane had gone through my office I had lost ninety-eight percent of my military plaques, awards, and coins that I felt were significant in my career. I wasn't stuck on myself; I had been encouraged to bring those items to work, as it would motivate other soldiers in moving forward to accomplish goals, achieve awards, and advance toward promotion. But, it was all gone now. I looked back and I had my fun and through the last obstacle, I had finished strong. It was time to let this be the final act.

The Final Act: My Work There Is Done

I got up from my very nice modernized office that overlooked the airport and walked next door to talk to my supervisor. I can't believe I am giving all this up: top of the line flat screen monitor, office with a cafeteria downstairs, conference room, a great team of junior and senior leaders, and soldiers. Look how well the soldiers are now training for their wartime mission.

I am getting ready to leave the soldiers who worked directly for me, the team that kept the 400 + military personnel records straight. Look how they have grown! Some of them had been working here at the Pentagon on September 11 when the top floor above them collapsed. I remember when we first arrived at this building, the practice alarm system would make them freeze in place or hit the floor. Now they are on top of everything. You know you have a good team when you do not have to be in the office for them to still carry on just as if you have never left, making critical assessment of the situation, identifying and resolving problems. I know how to laugh with them and they know how to laugh back and remain professional. I will miss them.

I knocked on the door and supervisor Sam invited me to sit down. I laid my typed paperwork for retirement on his desk and told him that it was time for me to retire. He asked, "Are you sure? You still have that 'kick butt' in you." I told him, "Yes, I am sure. I just want to go home now. Change from being a military Humvee wife and mom to a civilian wife and mom.

He chuckled and said, "If you mean it, do it, but if you are going to go back to work full time in the civilian sector you might as well have stayed in. Think about it, and let me know, and I will support your decision." I looked at him and gave him the paperwork. I was sure. This part of the journey was finished for me. I cannot guarantee that I will be a stay home mom forever, which is a respectable job within itself, but I know this part of my journey is over.

Postscript: A Legacy of Pride January 2008

Today, I received a letter from one of my soldiers. I am proud of the legacy that has passed from my favorite sergeant to myself, to this soldier, who is now passing it on to the men and women for whom she is responsible.

"Ms. Trina,

You just don't know you got me here. I was going to get out of the military when I was in Vermont.

I was a college dropout and I joined the service. I remember the day you sat us down at the conference room (Vermont). You told us to write down short-term goals and long-term goals. I did that to my soldiers this year. I told them to come up with short-term goals and long-term goals.

My long-term goal was to go to graduate school and I am just three classes away from graduation. My short-term goal was the Officer Candidate School. You might not remember this, but it was a really good way to set up the attainable goal. I was so fat and out of shape while I was in Vermont. I lost my weight and got in shape when I moved to Fort Bliss.

Once I was told by another soldier in Fort Jackson that I am a double minority and I have no place in the military. Here I am, still in, but I have to put up with a lot of mess.

I am happily divorced, and I attend women's fellowship every Friday. I will be back in from Iraq in March/April and going to Kansas for my advanced schooling.

You are the best military supervisor I ever had, believe it or not. This deployment has made me realize that I need to have strong senior leaders to make things successful, and it makes things kind of hard at times with this unique generation of soldiers.

Thank you so much for everything you have done for me. I really appreciate everything. Keep in touch and take care.

Investing is a journey, not a final destination.

Sincerely,

Captain Iam Free

9/11: Leadership Strategies of Survival (S.O.S)

How can the musing of a former military leader possibly be of any use to an upper or middle manager in the corporate or governmental world? The key is to focus on the trait both of you share in common: Leader. There are qualities that are common to all effective leaders, and it is not only possible, it is essential to acquire these qualities and master the principles that arise from them.

An excellent, effective leader is a strategic thinker, evaluating himself and his decision making process. There is a theory, DISC: which stands for Dominant, Inspiring, Steady, and Conscientious behavioral preferences, that says that each person has a behavioral preference from which he operates and makes decisions within his work environment or a specific situation (Marston, 1928). By examining oneself and determining which behavioral preference is the one you use most, it is possible to change your own behavior and understand the behavioral preferences of your employees. Good leaders know how to step outside their preferred communication style in order to best motivate employees who do not respond well to a particular type of leadership. Such a leader gathers expert knowledge of himself, his motivations, and the facts needed in his field, using that knowledge to bolster the decision-making process and build confidence and morale among employees.

Great leaders take care of the people who work for them. Whether this is referred to as coaching, training, mentoring, or support, employees will not place their trust until a leader demonstrates concern for their welfare and well-being. Excellent leaders ensure that employees have the skills, training, support, and materials needed to accomplish the task at hand.

People are the greatest asset in any business. Without people, there is no one to perform the tasks that enable a company to succeed. The most effective leader's model and practice primarily by the Platinum Rule "Treat others how they want to be treated"; while similarly operating by Golden Rule: "Treat others as you want to be treated." This requires that an excellent leader have an awareness of behavior and personality. Such a leader knows when to appeal to pride in a job well done, and when to remind an employee, whose commitment to the company is wavering, of an obligation to set a positive example as a mentor to their fellow employees. Sustaining good employees within an organization can be challenging. However, simple principles such as creating a friendly work environment where people want to come to work, respecting the input of personnel, and providing opportunity for professional growth are deterrents of personnel shortages.

Along with a focus on the importance of people, a truly effective leader has faith. Having faith means believing in something larger and more powerful than oneself. Whether that someone or something is God, Jesus Christ, one's country, one's company or branch of service, or just in fellowship of man, effective leaders believe in something. Therefore, a good leader is also a dream maker rather than a dream killer. Dream makers encourage others to reach beyond their personal limits. They encourage that each person they encounter put forth their best effort and use the full limits of their intelligence and creativity to set and achieve personal and organizational goals. Such a leader looks for things that will advance the cause or complete the task to even in the midst of obstacles.

Overtime leadership can take a tool and it is necessary to have a way to recharge the spirit when things get tough. Faith is the means to recharge our spiritual and emotional batteries. If I am down to my last reserves of strength, what makes me think that I have anything to offer an employee who feels that they are at the end of their rope? The answer is faith. Faith that since we are still here, alive on this earth I will eventually take this negative situation or setback in life and use this situation in a positive manner to help someone or for a greater purpose. Mothers against Drunk Drivers was birthed from a mother who made a vow on her deceased daughter death bed that she would do something about drunk driving which took away her young life.

In addition to faith, an excellent leader also has a sound sense of ethics and morality. Decisions must be made based on what will bring the greatest good for the greatest number, and on what will cause the least harm. A good leader will not put an employee in a position where he has to violate his personal ethics in order to complete a task. This guides another trait of good leadership: structuring a situation so that the employee makes the right choices.

Genuine, effective leaders are also diplomats. They know that there is a hierarchy that must be understood and respected before any action can be taken. They do not burn bridges; they build them. They take the time to find out the facts. What is happening now? Who is available for which task? How are "your" workers distinguished from everyone else? Who is acting as a buffer, helping you accomplish the task at hand? Who has made himself a barrier? What are that person's motives, and how can you turn that individual from barrier to buffer? And if you cannot convince someone to stop being a barrier, how and with whom can you build a bridge over or around him?

The most effective leader is willing to make tough decisions. Such a leader will do what it takes to get the job done, and will not buckle under pressure. He understands the strengths and weaknesses of each person in the company and is willing to do something to increase those strengths and offset weaknesses, training workers to respond appropriately to crisis before situations arise. A good leader knows when to lay everything on the line for a principle. His inner dialogue is, "I am willing to take a calculated risk, if I fail, at-least I know I had the confidence to fail forward. One of my favorite leadership experts, Author John C. Maxwell said, " Failing forward means turning your mistakes into stepping stones for success (Maxwell, 2000).

Finally, a good leader finds his own replacement, stepping aside when the time comes, knowing when he has brought a company as far as it can go. This requires grooming a replacement from the date he himself was hired.

There are many people who believe that leadership is a quality that you either have or you don't. "Good leaders are born, not made," has often been heard, but it simply isn't true. Excellent leadership arises from one's experiences as well as from the leadership modeling each employee receives. How one responds to various experiences depends on many factors: modeling from other leaders, both at one's own level and higher, training, opportunity to demonstrate leadership, and practice over time. Crisis provides opportunity for leadership, painful though the situation may be. The key is to ensure that leadership through a crisis accomplishes all of the tasks at hand while supporting the people involved. This enables both leaders and employees to move past the situation and return to functionality as soon as possible while maintaining their humanity. This transformational leadership is essential to retaining good employees, avoiding burnout, stopping loss of qualified personnel and preventing posttraumatic stress disorder.

In this part of the book, you will see that excellent leaders are indeed, made. There are fifteen very important qualities that define these leaders: strategic thinker, model and practice, seek mentorship, know your priorities, role modeling, be diplomatic, faith outlook, make tough decisions, lade effectively, flourish with humility, identify ineffective leadership, authentic leadership, maintain character and respect, clearly communicate, and lead with competence. Anyone can become a better leader by employing these fifteen qualities in their day-to-day relations with employees, superiors, and even within one's own family.

S.O.S #1: Strategic Thinker

A good leader is a strategic thinker, evaluating himself and his decision making process. Continual self-evaluation is crucial to making solid decisions. If we are not aware of ourselves, our needs as an individual and as a part of an organization, understand the needs and demands of our families, and the needs others have for our assistance, understanding, support, and validation, then we cannot function effectively. Now this may sound like a lot, but a strategic thinker is able to organize their priorities and work efficiently to maintain balance in life and work. This process begins with a self-evaluation.

Self-evaluation is a process, which must take place long before the time for the decision arrives. Words internalized within our mind will produce positive or negative results. You may not be able to control your environment, but you can control how you react to the environment. Our personal hopes, dreams, fears, anxieties, and prejudices can color our decision making process. Sometimes decisions are made only after so much hesitation that they are in effect, useless, or the decisions made are based on a snap judgment, with little thought to the effects the decision will have on the people around us. Both situations are indicators of morale killers, and in any organization, whether civilian or military, morale is the keystone of effective action. How do you see the people you work with? Do you consider them lazy, always trying to take advantage of the system, or do you see them as team players and intelligent contributors to the organization? How you see employees affects the daily results you will get at work?

Strategic thinkers know how to hold two contrasting thoughts in their heads at one time and make an effective decision for the overall good of the organization and personnel. "They have the predisposition and the capacity to hold in their heads two opposing ideas at once. And then, without panicking or simply settling for one alternative or the other, they're able to creatively resolve the tension between those two ideas by generating a new one that contains elements of the others but is superior to both." (Martin, 2007, para.1)

Leaders often find themselves being forced to make decisions while under extreme pressure during a crisis. Taking time to reflect, rather than reacting to the situation, results in better decision making. Like a mother on an airplane, we must don our own oxygen mask before putting our child's mask to his face. Mind you, employees are not children, but we have the same responsibility to support our employees as that mother has to care for her child. The "...suck it up and drive on..." mentality is, ineffective in management. Not only does it often demean and disrespect the employee whose needs are being swept aside, it can create a callousness that builds barriers between managers, leaders, and employees. Carried to an extreme, this mentality leads to an organization environment that is hostile to the needs of the individual employee and leadership. Such a situation is an ironclad potential that employees will leave the company to seek a work environment that does not require a surrender of basic humanity.

S.O.S.#2: Model and Practice

Good leaders operate under the Platinum Rule: "Treat others as they want to be treated." Most people have heard of the Golden Rule: "Do unto others as you would have them do unto you." But there is another rule that is also needed in a successful life, and effective leaders know that and make use of it daily. The Platinum Rule says, "Treat others as they want to be treated." This requires a higher standard than the Golden Rule, because it eliminates the excuse of failing to treat others fairly, because they did not treat us well. Effective leaders model this rule with employees, colleagues, leadership, management, acquaintances and family.

If I cannot, or will not, practice the Platinum Rule in my own family, I am not going to be consistent about practicing it in any other area of my life.

I have a responsibility to model leadership in a way, which will pass on the best practices that I have been taught by role models. Mistreating others, devaluing their opinions, or ignoring their human needs makes my leadership weak, not strong.

As a leader, I am not alone. I do not operate in a vacuum. Those I lead must have confidence that I will consider their humanity when I make decisions, or they may simply refuse to do what is necessary. All the threats in the world cannot necessarily bring a soldier from a bunker to charge the enemy in the face of his own possible destruction. Only the belief that if he does charge, he knows he is doing this for a greater cause, the risking his life, for life.

Further, few employees will be willing to put the needs of the company before their own needs or the needs of their families if that company consistently expects them to use their personal time and resources without some corresponding benefit to themselves and their families.

If one family member constantly puts his needs and ambitions above the needs of the family as a whole, the strain will reach a breaking point. It not uncommon to find children who become unruly, spouses straying, and the family, which is supposed to be a haven from the troubles of our daily lives in the world, becomes, instead, a battleground of competing personalities, each determined to get his share. Similarly, if an organizations puts their needs and ambitions above the needs of their employees the strain will reach a breaking point resulting in lost production, manpower, and financial revenue.

One of the contributors to separation from both the military and from private employment is repeated stress on family ties. Companies that expect their employees to be constantly on the move from place to place, or to spend extended amounts of time away from home are finding it harder and harder to retain productive people. The good news is like the military, progressive organizations find creative ways to help employees to meet the needs of their families (i.e. Childcare, healthcare, family leave) while working on their organization's goals. In my case, I knew that any evaluation of the current situation that did not include my family would not be complete. A leader with incomplete information makes poor decisions.

S.O.S.#3: Seek Mentorship

A person left to himself (alone) is subject to do anything (E. Reeves, personal communication, November 1, 2008).

If we lived in a perfect world, we would have perfect people, and perfect systems in place. Without some type of accountability people are capable of going astray. I am not surprised (nor am I happy) when I hear of a famous person, sports figure, or politically leader has committed an unethical, illegal, or immoral act. Okay, I am a little surprised, but only for a moment. Often, I wonder what led to their demise. Was it too much power, control, a woman or man, greed, or pride? Yes, a trace of one of these elements are often there. But I solicit to you, one key aspect that was missed is accountability. Who watches the watcher? Who is the watcher accountable too? Who speaks into your life and can guide you to move forward with goals, dreams, and aspiration? Who is speaking into your life when you begin to isolate yourself from others or lag in work performance? Who is there to hold the mirror up in your face when you tend to believe it is always someone else fault and never your own fault? Who is speaking to you when you think you are the only one going through what you are going through? Who is there to show you the contingency plan of personnel replacement when you think that so many people depend on you that you are not replaceable? Who is there to tell you it is okay to laugh and not holding yourself to an unrealistic expectation? The Mentor. Every employee and leader should have a tangible mentor that speaks to them and is watching out for their best investment, which is themselves.

You are a unique individual with a purpose and destiny to affect change in a sector of life, protect yourself by being accountable to someone who will tell you the truth, cover you when you need to be covered, and is willing to turn you in, if you get out of control.

A good leader knows when to appeal to pride in a job well done, and to remind an employee - whose commitment to the company is wavering - of an obligation to mentor their fellow employees. Mentoring is one of the most important stop-loss tools available to any leader. Pride in one's company, accomplishments and abilities, is what motivates employees. Employees who feel trusted, useful, and respected are more likely to remain with the company over the long haul. Morale is higher, both among the newer employees being mentored and among the more experienced employees. According to Dau (2004), Employee Assistance Counselor at the University of Minnesota:

"Research findings indicate that when the organization is seen as supportive, employees have less absenteeism, fewer work-family conflicts, and less job and life stress. Supportive management practices have a positive influence on organizational commitment, job satisfaction, productivity, and satisfaction with personal growth and development by employees.

In a study of thousands of employed people, Duxbury and Higgins (1997) identified the characteristics of supportive managers. Hallmarks include: "...mentoring (emphasis added)..."

Morale is higher among newer employees who receive mentoring because they are able to learn more quickly what is expected of them when correct actions and attitudes are modeled than when they have to guess what is correct. It is higher among the more experienced employees because they feel valued and respected. Their acquired knowledge and experiences become a legacy, which is passed uninterrupted from one employee to the next, instead of being lost when that employee retires or quits. Effective employees are identified, and mentoring is provided at each stage of their career to ensure that the time and money the company has spent training these people will not go to waste. Such mentoring results in the employee needing to think things through before leaving the company. This gives managers time to create strategies to retain employees whose commitment is wavering.

Mentoring and support beyond the office is a very effective tool for staff retention and stop-loss. A leader's willingness to break the "boss" wall and step into the employee's day to day world, rolling up his sleeves to dig right into the most difficult challenges facing that employee shows a level of caring that is guaranteed to inspire a desire to stay with the company at almost any cost. This does not mean going uninvited into an employee's private life, but it does mean doing everything, which can reasonably be done to accommodate that person's changing needs so that he can be freed of as much stress and anxiety as possible.

The goal is not to eliminate all stress because a moderate level of stress is good. Stress provides motivation to solve problems. Too much stress, however, can result in paralysis. As the employee is backed further into a corner, he develops a learned helplessness, relying more and more on higher authority to tell him what to do, instead of gaining the confidence to solve problems on his own.

A good leader must have an awareness of behavior and personality. Instead of simply sitting back and waiting until an employee slips away, a good leader will engage in dialogue to determine what is motivating the employee to separate from the company. He will note issues raised by the employee, and brainstorm solutions that meet the employee's stated needs for retaining the employee, as long as they are within reason and will not overly burden the company budget. A good leader will weigh budget considerations against the cost of the lost productivity of the employee, plus the cost of training a new employee, plus the lower productivity that a new employee will have during his or her learning curve. Often employers will find it far cheaper to accommodate the needs of the experienced employee once they calculate the true cost of turnover.

Burnout can cause you to lose your job and impair working relationships All jobs have stress, and not all stress is bad. But too many emotional blows without restocking your emotional and mental arsenal can reduce, or eliminate, your ability to respond to future blows. This is where a good leader steps into the situation. Aware at all times what stresses exist in the workplace, he does whatever is possible to reduce or eliminate them. Such a leader gets to know employees well enough to be aware of the stresses they may be facing professionally. Willing to prevent burnout and reduce stress, an effective leader is available at all reasonable hours, working continually to build trust among the team and open communication, in order for an employee to feel comfortable confiding issues that are affecting work performance.

The best treatment for stress disorders is prevention, coupled with early detection. The Coping & Stress Profile® is an excellent tool for workplace awareness purposes if used early in the employees career and followed by a second administration immediately after unexpected changes. This is not a clinical tool and should not be used for therapeutic purposes.

Early assessment of potential sources of stress in an employee's life can help leaders avert a crisis later. Built upon previous research on stress, the *Coping & Stress Profile*® is based on a theoretical model called the Multi system Assessment of Stress and Health (MASH) model. The profile is a unique, self-directed learning instrument providing feedback on stress and coping in four interconnecting areas: person's work environment, family, personal life, and with couples (Inscape, 1995). This instrument provides insights on how stress affects a person's life, work, and other areas of their life, and offers strategies for distressing.

This instrument can be administered at any time in an employee's career or you can take the assessment at home. Within the work environment it is important that before you offer this assessment or any other assessment that you check with your human resource department or convening authority to make sure that the instrument is authorized to be used within this organization and how the instrument is to be administered.

Having a baseline assessment early in one's career can be very useful. Administering the assessment after a crisis can reveal changes in an employee's ability to handle stress. A good leader will craft a response to these changes in employee stress levels, preventing a crisis resulting in ongoing trauma, or even post traumatic stress disorder.

Denial and shock is one of the stages of grief. It is also a sign of trauma. During and after any crisis, it is important to identify any employees or persons you know to be stressed, traumatized, or moving toward Post Traumatic Stress Disorder. PTSD is a complex topic, and writing about it could fill entire racks of a library. In the aftermath of a tragedy there may be many employees who need additional assistance making sense of their trauma. An institutional mind set, such as that in a large corporation or in the military, can sometimes make a situation worse for a traumatized employee. The expectation to "...suck it up and drive on..." in the face of horrific loss can sometimes result in an employee rebelling against the system. If the system pushes back hard enough, the employee could resort to sabotage, self-abusive coping tactics such as alcohol or drug abuse, suicide, or even homicide.

Timothy Moss is a Gulf War veteran, licensed mental health professional and Board Certified Diplomat, both in Clinical Social Work and with the American Academy of Experts in Traumatic Stress. In his own words, he has had the distinct privilege of providing professional psychotherapeutic services to survivors of military combat, sexual trauma, terrorist incidents and natural disasters, both while on active duty and within the Department of Veterans Affairs. He has found such work with this unique population to be both challenging and concomitantly rewarding.

According to Moss (2008), "Post Traumatic Stress Disorder, or PTSD, in general layman's terms, is a NORMAL response to an ABNORMAL event in one's life. It can be caused by witnessing, or by exposure to, psychological trauma such as military combat experiences, sexual assault or other life-threatening events."

According to the National Center for Post-Traumatic Stress Disorder, Department of Veterans Affairs: Fact Sheet (n. d.), "PTSD is an anxiety disorder that can occur following the experience of witnessing life-threatening events such as military combat, natural disasters, terrorist incidents, serious accidents, or violent personal assaults such as rape." (para.1)

Moss (2008) states that "...veterans and other survivors with PTSD experience a vast and varied range of psychological and psychosomatic symptoms..." which include:

* painful dreams and memories
* intense anxiety and depression
* disturbed sleep
* suicidal and hostile impulses
* difficulty getting close to others
* numbing of emotions

* social isolation
* trouble working or finding meaningful activities

After any tragic event, according to Elisabeth Kubler-Ross, there are several stages of grief: Denial, Anger, Bargaining, Depression, and Acceptance (Kubler-Ross, 1969). As the initial shock of a horrific event wears off, the first emotion expressed is anger. This is because victims and bystanders experience a physiological reaction: an elevation in adrenaline. Adrenaline is the hormone, which gives our bodies the signal to flee from harm, and the strength and stamina to do so. This adrenaline, however, does not disappear immediately. Unused adrenaline remains in the body and triggers an anger response. This response tends to cause the release of more adrenaline until the threat is identified and removed, or until the affected person succumbs to exhaustion. While asleep, the body finally removes the adrenaline that has built up in the affected person's system.

When an employee is in the anger stage, allow the person to express his anger and fear. Help him find positive ways to vent his anger, such as talking about his feelings, writing poems, essays, or journal entries; anything that will provide an outlet. If an employee is venting at work, take that person aside and talk in a soft, calming voice. Reassure the employee that he survived, and remind him of anything that will help him regain a sense of himself.

Remind those who show signs of trauma of loved ones who were able to escape the tragedy, children that they need to care for, whatever helps the person. At this stage people have a strong need to DO SOMETHING. Help guide them on what they can do: help in recovery and rebuilding operations, serve food to victims and volunteers helping with recovery efforts, whatever is in one's heart.

Once anger fades, and sometimes-even while still angry, denial begins. Denial is the body's way of shielding the mind from events that are so horrific that they overload one's ability to cope. A sense of unreality descends, and the affected person needs time to reconnect. Sticking to one's normal routine is the best way to pass through this stage. Even though it may result in a few people becoming upset, getting back to business as usual, as quickly as possible, is essential to both personal and as business wide recovery. Be sensitive to the needs of those who cannot simply "...suck it up and drive on..." however.

When the person is finally ready to deal with the tragedy, they will sometimes experience survivor guilt. Persons in this stage will make such statements as, "I'd give everything I have if only this hadn't happened. Why did so and so die and not I?" This is the stage Kubler-Ross refers to as bargaining. This stage also includes those who pray to their God with an "If you get me out of this, I'll serve you forever by doing whatever you want of me." This stage can lead to a return to anger and more bargaining if events continue to be uncertain and frightening.

As time passes, the impact of the event fades, the person works through the first three stages, and depression may begin. Depression results when a person cannot find adequate emotional support systems or cannot reconcile events with their self-concept, worldview, or value set. The person may have trouble sleeping, sleep too much, overeat, lose appetite, lose interest in things that they used to find pleasurable, cry, show irritation out of proportion to the situation, drink excessively or use drugs to numb the emotional or physical pain they are experiencing, and many other symptoms. Untreated depression may lead one to harm oneself or others. Anyone who shows more than three of these symptoms for more than three weeks may require additional help. Physicians, counselors, clergy, and psychologists may be able to help the person work through this stage to get to acceptance and closure.

Not all stress is bad, but stress is cumulative. Like the straw that broke the camel's back, a crisis may be just the final addition to an already overloaded employee. Employees experience stress work and outside of the work environment. Consider all these stressors of daily life:

The door rings around seven one Saturday morning. An unexpected doorbell might be one of two things: An official at the door to notify that a loved one has passed away or a certified letter a postal worker has bought, perhaps with good news. Mary, one of your employees, opened the front door to see who has rang the doorbell, so early. "Oh," the postal worker said, "I thought no one was home." Mary smiles slightly at the mail carrier, since she knows the postal worker personally, she thought this was an ironic statement to make. Mary, politely she takes the mail and thanks the postal worker. Looking at the front of the letter she noticed the return address was from the homeowner's mortgage company. Could it be a refund check?

Hmm. It does not have the color of the check in the front window. He opens the letter to see that his mortgage is behind. As a matter of fact, the company wants the house back. The hapless recipient is shocked to see the mortgage is in default.

"Honey, didn't we send in the mortgage payment with the rest of this month's bills?"

The homeowner thinks to himself, ""Is this not the same company that welcomed our business when the economy was booming? Now they send a repossession letter. "We're going to take your home; it's in default."

Instead of the news reporting about people robbing banks, they should show the real truth. "Look at Jim and Jane walk through the bank door; I am hiding my "gun:" adjustable mortgage rates and sub-prime lending, behind the desk, because I do not want my customers to know to know that I am about to rob them. Sell them services they do not need; offer them a flexible interest rate while the economy is good. Little does this happy couple know that when the relationship changes, their lenders' smiling faces become like pretzels as they squint their eyes and press their lips firmly in a frown, putting on their eye glasses. They now point out to you the fine print in the agreement.

"Look here, this is the fine print that says we can take your property and increase the interest rate if you are even one day late on one payment; that is right, late one day on one payment. See right there, line 452 paragraph 93a, Section 1.3.1."

Mobsters now, they get ready for their black-tie affairs, socializing, enjoying the fringe benefits of your foreclosure. Not their problem, it is just business. In defense of the banking industry, I am not talking about all bankers. I am just having a reflection moment about current banking experience. Is this stress? Will this homeowner shrug this off, or will he carry his worry and anxiety into the workplace?

Two years before, feeling pretty good about a booming housing market, where houses were flipping faster than pancakes at IHOP, this homeowner listened to the financial advisers who urged everyone to "...buy houses, buy property." The first home he buys is a starter home, which he turns into a rental property. The second home he buys is for himself and his family. Homes number three and four were gifts from in-laws who wanted to keep their home in the family. Since he can only live in one home at a time, he and his wife decide to get tenants in the other three homes. These homes aren't making much of a profit from renters, because the true story about renters is if a renter takes care of the property and pays the rent, in itself an oxymoron, it is a miracle. Equity is what benefits the homeowner. He uses the equity to get the next home, as a means to prepare himself and his family for retirement. Now, with housing prices crashing left and right due to shady trading practices in bank futures, this homeowner faces foreclosure on his property.

The economy has shifted so quickly that he cannot liquidate the property. He decides that he will sell the first home, since it was the least expensive and is in a great location. Surprise, surprise, tenants have practically destroyed the home that was managed by a well-known management company. Equity, the difference between the value of the property and the amount owed, has dropped, effectively wiping out what was intended to be a savings plan for retirement. Is this stress?

What effect would a change in company retirement benefits have on this employee's willingness to stay with the company if it were announced at this point? For some people, this is not stress, either because they choose to be in denial or because they choose not to embrace the effects that circumstances dictate they will have to embrace. A wise leader would consider this, speaking with employees before implementing any changes.

What about the Chief Executive Officer of the company that is affected by the economy, or the corporate board, or investors? From a management perspective, who would want to tell their company that they are going out of business? Employees will be angry and distressed. Investors will howl; heads will roll.

This employee, already filled with foreboding about the uncertain financial future, drives off to find peace by burying himself in work. That morning, he goes out the door with his family, gets in the car, turns the key, but the car does not start. Is this stress? It is, but only if he chooses to embrace the effects of the situation. He tells the children to go in the house to wait and makes a phone call to finds out whether he still has his American Automobile Association membership. Keeping the engine running after Triple-A arrives, he drives the car to the auto shop, where he puts in a new battery. How will he pay for it? Credit. He will deal with the gangsters at the bank next month. The rest of this month he and his kids will ride. He wonders, "Will they come for the BATTERY?"

This employee is not unique. Every other employee in the company has a similar story, a life filled with stressors: pregnancy, new marriages, relationship issues, sick children, elderly parents needing full time care, poor physical condition from spending all their time sitting at a desk, conflict with fellow employees and supervisors, inadequate pay, and to top it off, now the company is laying off workers while demanding more work from those who survive the cuts. What a time for a crisis to occur.

S.O.S#5: Know Your Priorities

A friend of mine, Reni, a manager in a Federal government position, sent this essay on the importance of priorities:

"When I think about the words, 'thriving while striving,' many things come to mind, because there have been some challenges that I thought would wipe me out, but God, when He says, 'I won't put any more on you than you can bear," truly means just that.

Working in leadership positions, you convince yourself that if you aren't hearing or seeing any problems, then everything is fine. This is a very faulty concept. Just because you aren't hearing about a problem, or seeing its immediate effects, does not mean that one does not exist. A truly effective manager investigates daily, even hourly if necessary, in order to prevent the development of problems before they grow too big to control. However, as parents, we managers can sometimes overlook trouble brewing in our own households.

I have a son who will be fifteen very soon, and from day one we have been very close. He was the kind of child who wanted me looking at him 24/7. I am sure some of it was because he was sick a lot, but even when he was happy, he has always needed me to be his cheerleader. This type of relationship can sometimes cloud our judgment.

One day I woke up and didn't know who this little boy was anymore, who used to be my son. He was getting failing grades because he didn't bother to take his work out of his book bag, even though he had it. This person lied, looking directly in my face, over something that as parents have to deal with! At the same time are we too busy working to remember the obligations of home?

Then things started getting even more challenging, since I had committed myself to spending extra time (the little that I had) working on charitable projects. Now my son was with me, but when I asked about homework and other things, instead of making sure everything was done, I was more involved in what I thought to be Good Charitable Things. Well, I was slowly losing my son to the computer, to influences from friends, to everything but my attention.

He really started getting in trouble a lot, failing tests so badly that it was just about impossible to correct. He got put out of school and had to be home bound for over a month, which only made a bad situation worse. As parents, we think if we make a drastic move, we will make things better, somehow. As many of us know, that is not what happens; we somehow manage to make the situation worse. This is true in management as well. As I think about work, a problem employee goofing off can be a real morale killer for everyone else. Allowing ourselves to be fooled by a happy-go-lucky exterior, pulling pranks and taking pratfalls, can conceal a real cancer in our organization's ability to get tasks accomplished.

We were back and forth in the principal's and superintendent's offices. The reason for this was because he had gotten in so much trouble, that his name became teacher's lounge talk. When that happens, a person can sometimes not have anything to do with a situation, but since he was there where things were happening, he automatically became the culprit.

Now let's remember that my son had opened the door to these accusation because he first started misbehaving. It is very important that, as managers, we hold employees accountable for their actions and the effects of their decisions on the company. Those employees who demonstrate that they are not able to self-regulate their actions should not be surprised to find themselves facing additional scrutiny. The key for us, as managers, is to be able to separate past behavior from our future expectations. Every employee should be held to the same high standards. Those who consistently choose not to uphold those standards should be reevaluated. As a parent and a leader I must evaluate and reevaluate my actions to determine if I contributed to the situation in a positive or negative manner.

When someone decides to get his act together and no one believes him or trusts him, he starts to lose self-esteem. This was happening to my son. As parents, we start trying to rebuild our children's self-esteem, even though in our hearts we may not really believe a change is taking place, but we don't want them to feel like failures because we know there are so many negative situations that can follow those thoughts. As managers, however, we find that self-esteem must come from being productive, not from feel-good jargon. In order to pull an employee back into the fold, it is necessary to first assign a mentor to demonstrate the correct procedures and policies to follow. We must also provide specific guidance, detailing expectations, training and feedback to obtain the goals of the organization. As with children, we must create an environment that builds the self-esteem of relationships between employer-employee and know our priorities.

S.O.S #6: Role Modeling

Effective leaders should set a positive and moralistic example for others emulate, and inspires others to reach their full potential. Key characteristics of role modeling include:

*Be trustworthy

*Performing their duties with excellence

*Promoting teamwork,

*Delegate where possible

* Listening to employees

*Maintaining high personal standards

*Work through challenges

*Providing opportunity for professional development

*Encourage and model balance

* Set a standard worthy of emulating

*Admit mistakes and learn from mistakes

Further, effective leaders teach employees to set long and short-term goals, and help each of them map out a course that will help reach that goal. By linking each employee's personal goals to the overall goals of the organization, employees become more satisfied in their positions and begin to see that doing their best for the company will result in greater rewards.

It is important to note here that role models are not perfect people and are willing to admit their shortcoming. Positive role models are not seeking personal limelight, their charisma and expert knowledge draws others to be attracted to their role.

It is also important that I mention that not all effective leaders are positive role model. Hitler was an effective leader and a role model to others. Gang leaders are effective leader and role models to members.

I am sure you have your own list whose would fall in this category, as well. Positive role models are moral and ethical individuals whose actions are legal.

I remain grateful for the role modeling I received while pursuing my dream of earning a Master's degree, and I take this opportunity to share my gratefulness. I was very fortunate to have encountered a number of Dream Makers, online professors, whose support and encouragement kept me from quitting college when the challenges of persevering to the end during 9/11 appeared more difficult than I thought I would be able to bear. When the last college course was finished all I could think of was that I was glad it was finished. .

But thanks to a role model who I had never saw in person, she worked with the college and me, so that I could reach the goal to completion. Yes, I walked across the stage and honestly, I felt like running and shouting. Thanks again, Dr. J.

Recently, while I applying to teach a class online, I had an opportunity to review a writing assignment on policy and procedures for a potential online teaching job and the prompt given was "How to Respond to a Student's Request for an Extension." My response to the prompt was not based on perception, but on personal experience and in accordance with the Faculty Manual. The prompt stated, "a student comes to a faculty member and asks, 'I am behind on my schoolwork; may I have an extension?'" I took a moment to reflect on the challenges experienced while completing my master's degree and the influence that my role model had on me.

Let me reflect for a moment. On the first occasion, I was finishing up the final project for a curriculum development class. After interviewing and researching about six or so private schools, I had all of my research data in a binder in my car. My family had decided to attend a well-known amusement park for a little family fun and to my utmost surprise, someone had broken into my car and stolen the binder. You see, the binder was inside a professional portfolio bag. Apparently, the intruder thought he was getting something of value. Personally, this binder was priceless. This six credit hour course was now absolutely down the drain.

With a sick and disappointed feeling, I sat at my computer, emailed my online professor and told her what had happened. With much empathy, her words rang across my email, "Don't worry Trina, we will give you an "I" for incomplete and you can have the summer to work on it. If you need more time, let us know. In fact, give me a call and we will come up with a strategy to assist you. I know school is getting ready to end so it will be hard to conduct the interviews, but I have some ideas."

In my opinion, this professor modeled "I care for the student; I want the student to succeed." The standards of the work were not compromised, but the professor understood that as a working adult with a family, sometimes we face unfortunate situations.

The second occasion happened on September 11, 2001. I had taken my schoolwork and textbook to the Pentagon with the hope that during lunch I could complete my homework. Well, as I stated in my biography, the plane went through my office.

I thought this next part was insignificant until now. Not only did the plane go through my office, but it also took my schoolwork and textbook with it. I emailed my online professor shortly thereafter and told my professor that I had a story to tell her about my homework. I said, "You will not believe what happened to me. I know you have heard people say '...the dog ate my homework,' but the plane actually went through my office." It is important to note, this was a different professor.

When I checked my email, there was an empathetic tone across her answering email. She said, "Trina, do you know what you just said?

The plane went through your office." Next, she told me not to worry about the homework, just give her a call. I tell you this professor was my Angel Online, as every week she coached, encouraged, and helped me to move forward when I was ready. She was not just helping me to move forward with getting my schoolwork accomplished; but she helped me move forward with life in the midst of challenges. Online school became like a safe haven to focus on something positive in the future. The online classroom was open 24/7 and provided flexibility that I needed to maintain balance between family and work. .

Was every day perfect, "No". Even so, there were a few more times where I fell behind in my schoolwork and at one point, I thought I would quit. Again there was the professor who said," Why don't you just take the week off and go to a nice hotel and rest? Do something nice for yourself; don't worry about the deadline right now; just do something for you."

But the one thing that I remembered during that time was as long as I knew I had an assignment to accomplish on a particular date and completed the assignment, I knew the rest of the world was moving forward and so was I.

The moral of this story is that I finished that class, and with some help I was able to graduate. Why? Because the professor understood Policy and Procedures, but was willing to work with as much leverage as possible to help this student finish successfully.

But Dr. J wasn't just finished with helping me through college. To my surprise, at the university awards ceremony Dr. J and the staff presented me with an award for Endurance. The award was called the St. Paul Award, given to students who faced incredible and unexpected challenges throughout their degree program.

Now, I am faced with making a decision to extend a courtesy of an extension to a student in need. According to the faculty manual, the student cannot request an extension beyond five weeks after the course has ended. However, in this question, it did not indicate whether the student is working after the course was completed or have any extenuating circumstances; therefore, I took the liberty to respond to the student in this manner, "Dear John, according to the faculty manual you are not allowed an extension beyond five weeks after course completion. However, since we are in week four of the extension period, you may have another week." The grey area of the manual provided the flexibility. I chose to give the student the benefit of the doubt where the guideline was in a grey area, because I modeled the role models. Later, I learned this was not the ideal response according to policy and procedure; however the response was sufficient enough to pass the test.

S.O.S 7: Be Diplomatic

Good leaders are diplomats. They know that there is a hierarchy that must be understood before any action can be taken. Resist the temptation to go into a new situation to immediately prove that you are in charge. The "...kicking butt and taking names" is the worst thing a new leader can do. Not only does it foster a climate of fear and mistrust leading to insubordination, it also fails to respect the existing order. This does not mean tolerating incompetence, passive resistance or outright sabotage, but it does mean examining the situation, creating alliances wherever possible, and giving respect and reward where it is due. It only takes one person above or below you to derail any progress you might have made had you chosen a less confrontational approach.

According to the Merriam-Webster Online Dictionary, diplomacy is "...skill in handling affairs without arousing hostility: TACT." Tact, in turn, is "...a keen sense of what to do or say in order to maintain good relations with others or avoid offense."

A skillful leader is one who understands that any words or actions, which cause someone to become defensive are counterproductive. Once someone is engaged in defending his personal view of himself and his own competence, or in protecting his territory, power, or influence, he is no longer listening. For anything meaningful to be accomplished, a new leader must first get to know the people with whom he will be working, establish trust, and discover the motivations and goals of both superiors and subordinates. Only then can any meaningful change take place.

Sometimes the situation requires keeping thoughts and knowledge of what is to come quiet until the time for action arrives. Too much information can quickly become rumor, whipping up fears and putting people on guard. When people are on guard, they are far more likely to resist change, even if that change is for their ultimate good.

The ability to persuade others of the necessity and wisdom of a particular course of action is an essential skill for any leader who wishes to be effective. It is not enough to present a plan of action and demand compliance. You may get an initial reaction that appears to be compliance, but it will be lip service at best. Effective leaders know that they must first establish trust between themselves and those they wish to persuade. To establish trust with supervisors, an effective leader must demonstrate a dedication to the goals and concerns of the company. Establishing trust with employees is accomplished by showing concern for the welfare and well-being of each individual. Only after establishing this sense of trust will it be possible to persuade people to take the necessary action.

In addition to the need to establish trust, employees and superiors alike must see that the leader in question is consistent. Does this leader say one thing and do another, or does he back up his words with actions? Can he be relied upon to keep his word? Will he provide support when it is needed, or will he leave employees and superiors hanging when he is needed most? This stage of the persuasion process is hardest for new leaders, as trust must be established over time, and the amount of time needed is determined by those whose trust is being sought, not by the one seeking it.

When I first arrived at the Pentagon and discovered the challenges and scope of my new duties, I realized immediately that the task could not be accomplished alone. Overcoming one's desire to do everything one's self is a key leadership skill. Without the ability to delegate, a leader will quickly find himself bogged down in petty details, performing routine tasks instead of providing the guidance and leadership needed to motivate employees to perform to their highest capacity. I set about getting to know my fifteen new supervisors, laying the groundwork for the bonds I would need in order to build bridges between the directorates, and identifying the choke points I would have to eliminate before my task could be accomplished.

S.O.S #8: Faith Outlook

I want to stop for a moment and talk about faith. Faith is one of the most important qualities a good leader possesses. Without faith, there is nothing to support you when something occurs that is larger than your ability to deal with it. All leaders have faith, whether it is in something or in nothing, will determine your ability to deal with a genuine crisis when everything else you believed to be true, powerful, and effective has failed.

Faith develops and changes over time. We may not consciously be aware of this process until our faith is challenged. It is then we may find ourselves surrendering a situation that seems too large to fathom or too hopeless to believe if we do not maintain faith.

As a little girl, I had always been fascinated by Christmas and had an awareness of faith. During the Christmas holiday, there would only be a few Christmas presents under the tree. Christmas Eve was exciting for me, because I knew that the next day was Jesus' Birthday. I would go outside, weather permitting, with my hat and gloves and walk down a small hill, which led to the back of our small home. With a spoon in one hand, and a cup of water in the other, I was ready to take part in my favorite tradition. Digging through the grass, I would get to the dirt and began to dig up enough dirt to make the form of a cake, adding water to make it look chocolaty.

Christmas was a special day, because I was told it was Jesus birthday. I didn't understand how Jesus and Santa Claus were related, but growing up in a poor family, the Santa Claus myth was exposed by my parents, who wanted me to know they really worked hard for the few things they got the family for Christmas. Yet nothing could replace this excitement of making Jesus a birthday cake, except tasting the cake. It did not matter how much I tried, it still tasted like dirt. I would tell Jesus an early happy birthday as I hid the cake out of sight, never to return to look to see if Jesus actually took the cake or not. It did not matter, because I just loved this Jesus.

At the age of twelve, I was baptized in water to be like this Jesus, I did not understand what I was doing. My mother said, "When you come up from the water, act like you are a little excited or do something." So I did, I just waved my hands around. I did not feel a thing; I just knew I loved this Jesus. I wanted to be like this Jesus who had great faith.

I remember that my elementary school was behind my house, up on a far hill. To get there I could take a short cut through the woods, if I wanted. However, I was not fond of the woods, so I would take the longer route back and forth to school. One day, when I was walking home from school, it began to rain. As I looked down at the ground, I noticed a picture of this Jesus. How could anyone lose a picture of Jesus? I took the picture and tucked it neatly in my jacket. Next, I stopped by the ice cream truck and got my ice cream. I checked, and Jesus was still safe. When I got home, I tucked Jesus neatly away in a book. Whenever I needed Jesus, I would just look at his picture. Growing up relatively poor, I needed my faith to get through those challenging situations.

I must admit that I really did not know who this Jesus was. When I went into the military, I would attend church on Sunday, because it was what I thought you were supposed to do. It did not matter if I had been out sinning (now I know what the true name of it was). I was one of the faithful to the church, because I just loved this Jesus.

When I say "this Jesus", some people might take offense to it. But that is how I saw this Jesus. One day in Germany, I invited this Jesus into my life, when the man who was giving the sermon (priest, pastor, clergy, minister, reverend) asked us to close our eyes and then he followed with the question, "If you want to have Jesus in your life, come forward to the front of the church."

Actually, it was a warehouse, but I understood what he meant. What happened next was just like the movies. There were two voices talking to me. It was like there was a little angel on the right that said, "Go forward, Dear." Then it was a just like there was a red fiery devil with a pitchfork, speaking into my other ear saying, "You better not go forward. You know you were in the club last night. You know what you did last night. What are you going to tell your boyfriend when you go home?"

My heart was racing as I could hear those accusations in my ear that tried to paralyze me with fear. I actually opened my mouth and said, "Shut up devil, you fooled me." I was really mad, because I realized I did not know 'this Jesus', so I went to the front of the warehouse that was serving as the church and invited this Jesus into my heart.

Several months later, I flew home from Germany to visit my family. I wanted to get my special picture of Jesus. Arriving home, I went to my special book and could not find this picture. I searched everywhere and asked my mother if she saw this picture. She let me know that she had left the room the way I had left it. Thank goodness that it was clean. When I took my return trip home on the plane, I had to ask Jesus, "What happened to the picture?" I asked him in my mind.

I heard a voice that said, "Trina, you do not need the picture of Jesus; you now have him in your heart." That is how I began my journey of faith. Somehow, no matter what I go through, I always feel I am not alone; I have Jesus in my heart. I think everybody has faith. Faith to believe in something or faith to believe it does not exist. The difference is, if you have faith to believe God exists, it provides hope for the future.

My personal faith in God is what kept me going through the September 11th experience. . I have a favorite Bible scripture that says in Psalm 91, he that dwells in the secret place of the most High shall abide under the shadow of the Almighty. I will say of the Lord, He is my refuge. Thou wilt not be afraid of the terror by night, nor the arrow that flieth by day (vs1-5). I had to use these scriptures, especially when I was confronted with the temptations to become fearful. I would say, I am not afraid because He that dwells…I am hidden by God.

And as previously stated, this does not mean that those who lost their lives on that day were not hidden. There is evil in this world and as long as there is evil, people will do bad and awful things. It means for this particular time in my life, I was chosen to be here for this junction. There is no certainty when one will leave this earth; the one thing we know for sure is that we will leave.

On that day, September 11, I was challenged, as the name of my God was associated with terrorism. It felt like a conspiracy to give God a bad name. The Jesus that I had accepted in my heart was being counterfeited. I had learned that you accept Jesus in your heart by believing that God sent his only Son into the world to forgive men of their sins. Whoever believed that Jesus died for our sins and accepted Him into their heart would have eternal life, after they died. That sounded like happily ever after to me-exactly what I desired.

The terrorism of September 11, blowing oneself up in the name of God, was like a slap in my face. This was the act of man, not the God that I know and have grown to love. The acts on that day did not represent anything that I had read in the books about Jesus. My heart goes out to all the families and friends affected by this event. May you be strengthened daily to find peace, if you have not found it yet, and do not let evil actions cause you to ruin your lives. As a leader, surrender does not come naturally. We learn over time that there is a method or policy to apply to a given situation that is supposed to solve the issue. But when true crisis exceeds our abilities, whether this is due to shock, the chaos of the moment, faltering courage or injury, there are sometimes situations that we cannot handle on our own, or even with the help of employees and fellow leaders. That is when we must maintain a faith outlook.

S.O.S #9: Make Tough Decision

Replacing key personnel is essential to recovery following a disaster. Although you and your staff may want to continue to grieve, you must begin to move forward. One of the more devastating effects of the September 11 tragedies was the death of such a large number of top people in their fields. Not only were these talented people lost, there was no one of their caliber available to replace them. Anyone who might have considered going into one of the affected fields thought very hard about it, and many decided to go into other fields instead, further reducing the pool of available replacements. Consequently, hiring temporary replacements for key positions became looming options.

Effective leaders will acknowledge grief while demanding adjustment to the new situation. Both experienced staff and the new, temporary staff must be supported during the transitional period. They will assist in building bridges between experienced staff and temporary staff, providing intentional opportunities for the two groups to learn to trust and rely upon one another.

After such an incredible loss, it is difficult to imagine intentionally sending personnel into hazardous situations, but that is exactly what an effective leader must be prepared to do. Shielding workers does them no favors. September 11, 2001 also provided a graphic demonstration of the need for physical fitness, emotional resilience, and courage from all workers everywhere, not just those in the military. From generals at the Pentagon to food service workers in the World Trade Center Towers, every employee needs to be assertive in maintaining readiness for the unexpected.

Physical fitness is an area that successful leaders also need to encourage. There are many occupations in which employees are expected to be physically fit as a matter of course: the military, firefighters, police, and emergency rescue workers must be able to perform certain physical tasks in order to continue employment in their given field. We don't really think of office workers, teachers, hairdressers, shopkeepers, or restaurant staff as needing to be physically fit. Many of them may never be in a situation that is as life threatening as the September 11 attack on the World Trade Center towers, but it is impossible to ignore the fact that many individuals who did not escape the towers were slowed by people ahead of them who could not navigate flight after flight of stairs. Companies, which acknowledge this necessity should implement on site physical fitness plans and actively encourage employees to participate in them.

Whether the company is willing to go to the expense of a fitness plan, managers cannot delude themselves about the need to brainstorm worst-case evacuation plans for their buildings. No longer can leadership bury their heads in a grandfather clause for a building that is not accessible and escapable by all. Deficiencies in a building must be corrected or personnel moved to a more accessible section of the building to assure their ability to safely exit in an emergency. Alarm systems must be tested to make sure that every employee can see, feel or hear that the system has been activated.

Further, evacuation plans should not be just a diagram on the wall. They should be practiced regularly. With a complete critique afterward, that includes brainstorming remedies for anything, which prevents the safe and orderly exit of every person from the building. These remedies must include the firing of anyone who refuses to take evacuation plans seriously.

S.O.S #10: Lead Effectively

From reading the work of James McGregor Burns, I have learned that there are two types of leaders: transformational and transactional (Burns, 1978). Transformational leaders offer a transcendent purpose as their mission, addressing the higher order needs of followers, such as nurturing, guidance, and role modeling. They understand that the dreams and goals, which give the most satisfaction are the ones with some risk involved in them. Thus, transformational leaders make sure that there is a higher cause at stake when making assignments. The knowledge that failure has a greater price than just our time is a great motivator. Transactional leaders, on the other hand, provide tasks, sometimes just to keep employees busy, without engaging subordinates in the larger picture.

Transformational leaders come with an extremely important set of skills that makes them effective at pulling employees into their vision: charisma, inspiration, intellectual stimulation, and individualized consideration.

Paul Graham, in an essay written in November 2004, states that charisma includes being "...confident, cheerful and outgoing, but especially outgoing." The most charismatic leaders, then, are the ones who truly enjoy people and cannot help letting that enjoyment show. That feeling of hospitality and approachability they give to relationships results in them inspiring cooperation in subordinates.

Effective, transformational leaders provide intellectual stimulation as well as emotional appeal. They demonstrate a respect for the intelligence of those around them by challenging followers to use their own ingenuity to solve problems, and by providing assignments that require critical thinking and creative problem solving strategies.

Pendergrass, my second military supervisor, was absolutely a transformational leader, breaking through the core of cynicism and minimal effort that had come to define my attitude toward my military career. He led by example. Pendergrass was one of the first leaders I encountered who made it his personal responsibility to ensure that his subordinates had the guidance, training and tools to complete each task. In return, he expected those he led to do what they were supposed to do. Everyone was expected to put forth their best effort, rather than simply rush through a task. He modeled going the extra mile, taking the time to "...put the shine on..." before considering a task completed. This provided challenges to match or exceed his examples.

Thanks to this excellent leader I learned to become more self-disciplined instead of doing just enough to keep supervisors off my back. I began to take pride in being my personal best at all times, and to caring more for the image I projected to supervisors and fellow soldiers. I now pay attention to the small details that I had previously given short shrift, and the quality of my work, even my personal appearance, improved. I began to be noticed for my own excellence, and to take pride in it.

Good leaders practice transformational leadership. Leadership role models are essential in developing the character and technical proficiency of future leaders. Over the years, I can recall only a couple of leadership role models that I would want to emulate. Specifically, the two role models I can recall into my military career at strategic seasons when I needed intense guidance. As quickly as they came into my career, they accomplished their goals and disappeared. Both leaders accomplished their mission while looking out for the welfare of this now retired soldier.

I would like to address the characteristics of transformational leadership displayed by one of these two role models. He was definitely a transformational leader and wherever he and his family currently reside, I wish them nothing less than the best.

S.O.S# 11. Flourish with Humility

Insert from Senior Military Leader and Friend

Great leaders can absolutely flourish during difficult times, as long as they pay constant attention to their internal mirror, window, and crystal ball. How we see ourselves, others, and situations acutely impacts whether adversity wins or we use it to push, prod, and propel ourselves into destiny. Our internal vantage point can mean the difference between thriving or barely surviving. A thriving leader frequently checks his internal mirror and makes adjustments when necessary, maintains a proper perspective when observing others, and sees past the current difficult moment into the future.

After completing a successful career in the military, I am now engaged in the business of developing future leaders and executives. Having had ample opportunity to observe great leaders, mediocre leaders, and poor leaders, I am convinced there is a need to renew and fine-tune their executive skills. Great leaders thrive under pressure because they are comfortable with themselves. They are comfortable with themselves because they have raised their level of self-awareness by gazing into their internal mirror. They understand, not just know, their strengths and weaknesses and are comfortable being in charge.

Being in charge does not make one perfect or all knowing. A great leader is humble, can accept wise counsel and often chooses to listen rather than be heard. After all, if the leader takes time to look in his internal mirror, then one can be sure of what is known and what is unknown. When it comes to the things leaders do not know, they can only learn them by actively listening and observing. Everyone around the leader knows something the leader does not know, and a great leader figures out what those things are.

When leaders are comfortable with themselves, it helps others to become more comfortable with their particular leadership style. Fidgety leaders typically breed fidgety environments, which often results in uncomfortable and chaotic organizational climates. Comfortable leaders are at ease with their own decision-making process and are able to help steady the ship as it sails through rough waters.

It is vital that every leader understands himself, his preferences and decision-making processes, and the lenses through which he looks: why he thinks the way he thinks. This information assists the leader in improving his understanding of what is really happening, which is typically more than meets the eye.

Any leader can become a better leader by looking into his or her internal mirror first. He should constantly ask himself questions. "What do I see? No, what do I really see? Who am I? What do I believe? Why do I believe what I believe? What motivates and fulfills me, and why is this so? Where am I going, and why am I going there? How will I know when I am there? What about others? Who and what is important to me? Why?" Such personal reflection helps the leader transmit strength during chaotic situations.

Critical reflection helps leaders to self regulate attitude and actions during crisis and chaos. Someone once stated that insanity is doing the same old thing, but expecting a different outcome. Great leaders can accomplish self-regulation by challenging their inner assumptions. Challenging these assumptions assists effective leaders in finding the best solution to the problem at hand. Great leaders go beyond the surface of a problem to ensure that they understand the entire situation. A quick glance does not always reveal the whole truth, nor lend itself to proper resolution of a chaotic situation. Creative solutions are birthed through critical reflection.

Great leaders don't have to toot their own horns or be the focal point of a staff meeting. They respect the experience and value which each team member brings to the table. Poor leaders tend to micro-manage, creating a climate of intimidation and distrust. Teams thrive when members know that their opinion is valued. A comfortable leader encourages participation and builds the team. The comfortable leader may say the least during the meeting. After all, efficiency and effectiveness are the ultimate objectives of a great leader, not being heard.

When leaders like what they see in the mirror, it increases self-confidence. Self-confidence helps leaders maintain their composure when chaos erupts, and it seems like all hell is breaking loose. Leaders' perspectives and analysis during difficult times are shaped by their vantage point or the internal window from which the chaos is observed. Is the glass half-empty or half full?

Chaotic situations could be an indicator that new beginnings are on the horizon. While one chapter may be ending; what new chapter could be unfolding? Great leaders don't let the things they see destroy their vision. A great leader understands that what appears obtrusive doesn't mean the end of destiny. Great leaders find another way to make their vision happen, even if it means starting all over again. New starts mean the leader has gained experience and has an opportunity to make the next time even better. A new beginning could be the very action that will stifle the chaos. While every action triggers a reaction, the proper response will always be a part of the solution and not the problem. Peace and comfort can simultaneously accompany heartache and sorrow, if allowed.

Great leaders understand that tragedy brings with it opportunity for new beginnings and possibilities. Opportunity knocks during chaos, and the leader who seizes the opportunity can capitalize from the moment. Leaders can choose to see the chaotic situation as only a moment in time to show their unflinching courage . The chaotic situation could be the squeeze that reveals what is inside that leader. Greatness is achieved when leaders are tested beyond their perceived capabilities. Leaders should choose to see chaos as an opportunity to excel.

It is not only important that leaders look in the mirror to be certain they understand themselves as they endeavor to properly assess the situation, but it is also important that leaders carefully look out their window in order to properly understand people. Chaotic situations generally allude to the possibility that people's behavior may spiral out of kilter. Chaos brings out the worst and the best in people. Many times people's fears and assumptions are demonstrated by their actions.

Their actions, however, should never result in improper reactions by the leader. Great leaders set the example.

People generally vent because of their insecurity, worry, or feelings of intimidation in relation to the situation at hand. A wise leader does not allow someone else's fear to become his. Insensitive outbursts are usually a sign of insecurity and/or a cry for help. That person's peace of mind is disrupted, and he is trying to influence others' situations. The leader can help to calm the persons' fears or become a companion and look for others to join in a calming response to the situation. The proper response by the leader can restore the chaotic situation.

Leaders' best decisions are generally made after a time of reflection. Routinely, all leaders should take time out to reflect upon matters at hand. Reflection helps a leader to separate the problem's symptoms from the real problem itself. Resolving a symptom of a problem will not solve the problem and could make matters even worse. Chaos requires sound decision making from good leaders to help restore positive good order and discipline. Great leaders accept the challenge to restore order because they have a sense of duty and commitment of their will.

In conclusion, not only can adversity be viewed as a temporary schoolmaster to prepare leaders for the road ahead, but also as great preparation for additional responsibility. Adversity teaches leaders that they are made of the right stuff to handle crisis situations. It also teaches leaders how to properly handle chaotic events. Chaos stretches leaders' comfort zones and makes them more versatile. Triumph through chaos builds confidence. If a task has been accomplished once, the task can be accomplished again. It could be completed even more effectively the next time by learning from previous experience.

Experience is the best teacher. While great leaders look back to the lessons they learned to help them when dealing with chaos, they look forward to tomorrow and what could be to motivate themselves and others. They don't just look back to the past or only at the current situation, they look inside their internal crystal ball to see a brighter tomorrow. Great leaders are visionaries and have the ability to look into the future and see change coming. Leaders should expect and anticipate change. Great leaders always move forward.

Great leaders understand that everything must change and trouble doesn't last forever. Just as seasons come and go, chaotic situations too will come and go. Many have missed out on great opportunities and investments because they threw in the towel too soon. Others have had the wisdom and discipline to weather the storm, make adjustments when necessary, and have gone on to become very successful.

I have observed that great leaders thrive through chaos because they are comfortable with themselves and have accepted their leadership role. They understand their limitations and their vantage point. They are not rattled by current situations or people, but choose to view adversity as temporary, as an opportunity to make a difference. They change what they see by gazing into the future and moving forward. Great leaders thrive through chaos because they choose to look beyond the present circumstances. What do you see? Look again.

S.O.S #11: Identify Ineffective Leadership

In 1984, at the age of twenty, I was stationed in a military transportation company located in Mannheim, Germany. Excitement was far from my mind, since my previous job assignment had left a bitter feeling inside me. Poor leadership had contributed greatly to my bad attitude and negative perception of the military. Often, my mind would reflect on the numerous times I had been left unsupervised, outside in the bitter Oklahoma winter, performing preventive maintenance care on military vehicles and associated equipment. Oklahoma had been my first military duty station. All the things I previously had been taught about noncommissioned officer (sergeants) leadership in basic training were quickly dispelled as my lazy and lethargic leaders would maintain their command position in a warm building, eating donuts and drinking coffee. Harassment and discrimination against women were prevalent, but with the intentional closure of their eyes, these worthless leaders considered it to be an expected part of indoctrination into the organization.

Arguably, the military was struggling at the time with the integration of women into its ranks. Women composed a mere two percent of the military in 1972 and twenty years later women composed only 13.5 percent, a mere fraction of male forces. The old training methods that had been so effective when training men were not as effective with women. Humiliation and hazing, believed to "make men from mama's boys," easily spill over into misunderstandings, threats, sexual harassment, and even outright rape, as recent headlines attest. Stricter guidelines are in place today and there are reporting channels to assist soldiers in order to eliminate such tactics.

S.O.S #12: Authentic Leadership

Research strongly suggests that worker performance, job satisfaction, and retention of workers are all influenced by a positive relationship with one's immediate supervisor. I did not have a very positive relationship with my first permanent military supervisor. "The importance of meaningful work and engaging experiences becomes more critical for organizations to consider given recent research indicating employee intentions to quit once the economy and job market improves." (Scroggins, 2008, para. 3).

From my first experience at this job, I had developed a very bad attitude toward work. I was often left unsupervised as a new soldier and had to read manuals to figure out how to get my job done. I remember one particular day, it was raining and my supervisor sent me outside in the "pouring rain" to check out the military vehicles. When I came back inside, I was soaking wet and cold. He was nice and dry, eating donuts and drinking coffee. I remember my stepfather always told me "Not to take any wooden nickels," somehow what I was experiencing wasn't genuine. After a year of lack of authentic leadership, internally I had given up at work. Authentic leadership means taking a genuine interest in showing someone how to be the best they can be, with the knowledge they have and the knowledge you have.

When it was time to leave this military job and go overseas to Germany, somebody really was watching. The commander made sure I left with an award and promotion. Yet, that was not my reward system for motivation back then and my morale was down when I arrived in Germany.

For example, I would put just enough work effort into my job not to get in trouble. I wore my military uniform wrinkled, with dirty boots, and I was borderline insubordinate.

My next new leader, Pendergrass, was a conscientious professional who tried to reach out to understand what was wrong with me. Honestly, at the time, I had given up. In my perception, all leaders were the same: untrustworthy. I just looked forward to Fridays so that I could hang out with my friends. After two months of this ridiculous behavior, Pendergrass sat down and counseled with me, telling me he could "...see so much potential in me and could help me, if I would allow him."

He informed me that although he would be separating from the military within a year, he would teach me everything I needed to know to be a good soldier. This transformational leader lived by the military noncommissioned officers' creed, an oath that emphasized multiple leadership traits of an excellent leader.

Since I had planned on getting married eventually, Pendergrass ensured that I obtained adequate housing and transportation. In the past, personal relationships were taboo. However, I could tell by Pendergrass's leadership in assisting married couples that times were beginning to change. The Army had come out with a married couples' program, designed to keep married couples together. Previously, the underlying tone was that the military did not issue you a family. The military began to take a more progressive perspective on family readiness and continues to work with soldiers and their families. Similarly today, corporate American and government organizations have begun to change, becoming more family and couple friendly.

Tsadik (2007) cited sixty-five percent of women in executive positions at their company are working mothers.

Today it is not uncommon to find companies that offer eight weeks of paid maternity leave and up to three years of unpaid leave to its women employees. Further, it not uncommon to find companies allowing new mothers to work part-time from home and gives them access to childcare centers near the office or on site. Fathers have also begun to be offered time off after a wife's pregnancy, as well as time off to take care of a seriously ill family member.

The Ideal: The Leadership Creed

Pendergrass modeled the principles expressed by the Noncommissioned Officers' Creed (NCO). "No one is more professional than I. I am a Noncommissioned Officer, a leader of soldiers. As a Noncommissioned Officer, I realize that I am a member of a time honored corps, which is known as "The Backbone of the Army". (NCO Creed, 2005, para.1) .The NCO Creed provided an informal measuring device to reinforce the values and expectations these leaders were supposed to embody. Two things that a Noncommissioned officer keeps focused on is accomplishing the mission and the welfare of their soldiers. This ideal leadership creed works effectively in corporate, business, government, and private sector.

Pendergrass displayed key characteristics of the Noncommissioned Officers' Leadership Creed, including authentic leadership, good moral character, effective communication, competence, role modeling, ethics, ability to accomplish any given mission, ability to provide appropriate support to soldiers, knowledge of his soldiers and their motivations, technical expert knowledge and tactical proficiency, selfless service, ability to exercise authority and power appropriately, respect, integrity, and moral courage. I will examine three of my favorite characteristics demonstrated through Pendergrass's leadership: Character, Communication, and Competence, which I deemed extremely important.

S.O.S. #13: Maintain Character and Respect

According to the Merriam-Webster Dictionary, character is the compilation of mental and ethical traits marking and often individualizing a person, group, or nation. Excellent leaders model good character, developing it in others by their example. Morale is highest when employees know that good character is encouraged and rewarded. According to the Josephson Institute, there are six pillars of character: trustworthiness, respect, responsibility, fairness, caring and citizenship.

Effective leaders establish trust by being consistent and doing what they say they are going to do. They do not simply give an order and go away, ignoring the needs of their staff. Instead, they roll up their sleeves and work right alongside, providing an example of what is expected, giving guidance and support so that the task at hand is accomplished and resources can be moved to the next problem as soon as possible. Their trustworthiness engenders respect.

Respect is a two way street. Effective leaders do not demand respect; they earn it. By following the Platinum Rule, "treat others as they wish to be treated," leaders ensure that every encounter leaves each employee feeling trusted and valued as a person. Effective leaders give responsibilities to each employee in accordance with his ability. Rather than micromanaging outcomes, the most effective leaders allow followers to brainstorm solutions. This demonstration of respect for an employee's intelligence and ingenuity provides an intrinsic reward for "out of the box" problem solving.

Another way excellent leaders earn respect is by being tolerant of individual differences. No two people have the exact same skill set, nor do they have the exact same competence. Excellent leaders do not focus on shortcomings, but on strengths. When forming task groups, these leaders consider which skills will be most essential to the task at hand. Each team member may have one or more of the necessary skills, and must work together and share their expertise. This gives each employee the opportunity to put forth his or her best effort where it will have the greatest effect.

Effective leaders are considerate of the feelings of others. They use persuasion, not threats, to accomplish tasks and motivate employees. Rather than meeting sarcasm with sarcasm, anger with anger, or insults with insults, an effective leader deals peacefully with disagreements. Each encounter is carefully crafted to prevent backing an employee into a corner. The most effective leader will listen twice as much as he talks, and will validate the employee's concerns and fears before proceeding to his own view of the situation. This respect blunts any further bad feeling, and often results in winning an employee back to the company's side.

Again, the first lines of the NCO Creed read, "No one is more professional than I. I am a Noncommissioned Officer, a leader of soldiers." (NCO Creed, 2005, para. 1) Leaders are the people who decide what needs to be done and the ones who make things happen. Truly good leaders know how to get the most from employees, not through threats or coercion, but through persuasion. Each leader has a behavioral preference from which he or she operates and from which decisions are made, but good leaders know how to step outside their preferred style when necessary, in order to best motivate employees who do not respond well to that particular type of leadership. Leadership is accomplished by sizing up the current situation and mobilizing an appropriate response.

Pendergrass's initial response to my lackluster performance was to determine the cause of my misbehavior instead of simply overreacting to my behavior. He used his technical and strategic knowledge and experience to outline a corrective course of action to save a military personnel asset instead of immediately recommending punishment. Pendergrass's form of correction avoided using an accusatory tone, provide a clear plan for immediate improvement, and kept counseling notes of measured progress. Pendergrass chose the situational approach to leadership, which emphasizes that there is no one best way to influence followers; the management style to use is based on the cooperation of the follower in a given situation.

S.O.S. #14: Clear Communicator

Effective leaders are good communicators; truly skillful leaders ensure that they use the right mode of communication with a given person. Everyone has a communication style that they prefer. It is not at all effective to use email or texting with someone who likes to speak face to face, nor to speak bluntly with someone who prefers to avoid conflict. Pendergrass understood that communication was a powerful means for establishing and maintaining trust. Effective communicators are able to build a bridge that transmits the behavioral intent of the organization to followers, creating the foundation for trust. By talking to me, asking questions, and paying attention to my answers, Pendergrass laid the foundations for a newly formed trust that supervisors would actually provide support rather than just give orders and go off to a comfortable place to wait until the next time they feel the need to shake things up.

According to Sarah Edelman and Louise Remond, there are three communication styles: aggressive, passive, and assertive. Aggressive communication is characterized by the use of blaming, labeling and sarcasm. Aggressive communicators are more concerned with getting their point across than in coming to a meeting of the minds. Such communications leave the listener feeling devalued, ignored, or put down.

Passive communication, on the other hand, is characterized by fear, shame or embarrassment. Rather than spelling out their wants and needs, passive communicators expect others to be mind readers. When their own needs remain unmet for a long enough time, passive communicators become resentful. This resentment eventually reaches a boiling point, and they lash out, screaming, accusing, and making the situation even worse.

Assertive communication, however, is a two way street. Assertive communicators are able to express their wants and needs while remaining respectful of the needs of others.

Assertive communications skills are vital to any manager. Each person states his wants and needs, then listens to learn what the other person wants. A manager must communicate orders to employees in such a way that the orders he gives are carried out quickly, correctly and effectively. Each searches for common ground. Both parties brainstorm possible solutions that will resolve the situation in a way that satisfies the needs of both individuals. A manager's method of communication will determine how he will be perceived by his employees, and how his orders will be implemented. For example:

The windows of a store need to be cleaned so that the storefront is attractive and appealing to passing customers. Manager A approaches two employees and tells them, "Y'all need to be cleaning these windows, instead of just standing there like that," and walks away. This is an example of aggressive communication. The manager in question has just made these two employees feel like they are not appreciated. By not asking whether there was a reason they were "...standing there..." this manager has indirectly accused the employees of incompetence. The employees realize that the gruff statement was actually an order, and are irritated at how it was given. They take their time "finding" the supplies to clean the windows, give them a quick once over, not really caring how they look, and call the task finished. However, the windows now have smears and are still unattractive. The job was not done well because it was not communicated effectively.

Manager V also sees that the windows need to be cleaned. He approaches the same two employees and remarks, "Man, these windows aren't looking good. Would you want to shop anywhere where the windows look like that? How about you two finish up whatever you are doing and take care of these for me? Thanks!"

Manager V has effectively communicated to these employees exactly what he wants done and why it matters. Since he spoke to them in a more respectful manner, they are happy to go find the supplies and take pride in cleaning the windows thoroughly. This manager has demonstrated that he is aware that the two may actually have a legitimate reason for what they are doing. He thanks them for completing their original task, as well as for listening about the new task. These employees now feel appreciated, so they do a better job. They are also motivated to look around and see what else they can accomplish, in order to continue to receive reinforcement that is more positive.

S.O.S. #15: Lead with Competence

Competence is a vital quality in managers. From the company's standpoint, competent people are needed in order to lead employees effectively and achieve higher profits. From the employee's perspective, having competent management is also vital. An employee needs to be able to rely, with no reservations, on management decisions in order to work effectively. Doubts about the manager's competence create conflicts ranging from minor acts of insubordination to outright resignation.

Employees can sense incompetence the way a wolf can sense a sick deer. Much like the deer is devoured by the wolf, the manager will find himself devoured by the employees who sense his incompetence. He will be unable to command respect, and therefore unable to get his orders carried out promptly and effectively. Incompetent management places doubts in the minds of the employees: "Should I REALLY go do what Mr.. Manager asked? Is that the best way to get the job done? Does he even know what he's talking about? Maybe I should wait until the next manager comes on shift and ask. Maybe I should find another job." These unspoken thoughts are why it is vital that managers appear competent at all times to their employees. In a time-sensitive situation, hesitation on the part of employees can make the difference between the success or failure of a given project.

How does a manager appear competent? Knowing about the company and your role in it is one important step. What decisions are you responsible for making? What orders should you be giving? What issues should you be leaving to a higher authority? What details should you ignore, allowing employees to decide how to effectively operate within standards?

A manager also needs to know his employees: what their job duties include and exclude, how each person works best. For example, a restaurant manager who sees a server who is shy and speaks too quietly for guests to hear easily might shift that employee to the dish room. Conversely, seeing a dishwasher who is friendly with guests and seems to get a lot of attention, that manager may feel the employee's talents are better used as a server.

A manager must appear confident with his decisions. When questioned, a manager should either answer confidently or admit that he does not know, and will look into finding out. This, of course, MUST be followed up by actually finding out. Doing what you say you will do is an essential part of competence.

Here is an example of what can happen when employees perceive that you are an incompetent manager:

Manager J talks and jokes with his employees throughout the day, even during closing time, when he should be out checking to be sure that all nightly cleaning duties are finished. Since the employees know that J will most likely be in some part of the restaurant telling a long-winded joke, they can either do their work slowly, "milking the clock" for extra pay, or they can do it shoddily, not completing things they don't feel like doing. J won't notice because he will be talking until the employees come and tell him that everything is finished and they will be leaving. In the morning, when manager V comes onto the shift, he will see that the dining room was not properly swept the night before, the tables are in disarray, and someone has left dirty towels from the night before on the server line.

V is a competent manager and knows he wants to run a smooth shift. Now he is faced with the unpleasant task of asking his opening employees to fix the mess left from last night, a shift that had nothing to do with them. However, V is a competent manager who commands the respect of his employees so they will follow his orders. They will not be upset with V that he asked them to clean up after last night's shift. However, you can bet that they will find out who worked the night before, including manager J, and be angry with those people. J will then appear to employees to be even more incompetent, which will further worsen this cycle.

Competence was Pendergrass's watchword. Competence is the expectation that a person is able to get things done for the business unit with a winning record of accomplishment. Work must be complete and accurate, with no part of the task left undone. Expertise in leadership skills is another dimension of competence, which is the ability to challenge, inspire, enable, act as a role model, and encourage followers.

After Pendergrass's assessment of my professional potential, I was assigned a trainer to quiz me on promotions and soldiers' competition boards. Experienced peers were assigned to teach me how to perform my job, followed by Pendergrass's expert training for all of the soldiers, myself included, on workplace and military equipment. Female mentoring provided me with a better understanding of the proper wear of various military, professional and workplace garments, as well as personal equipment.

Another aspect of competent leadership is training employees in the importance of following policy. A policy is a plan or course of action intended to influence and determine decisions and actions, which was adopted because it was considered expedient, prudent, or advantageous. From the sole proprietorship to the international corporation, every company relies on policies every day to carry out its business. Management and employees alike must always strive for compliance to policy. Policies are put in place as plans for how to handle certain issues or situations. They are either planned in advance, or altered and adopted when the need becomes apparent. In either case, policy is made when there is time to think. Policies are there to be followed when in the thick of a situation. They are there to guide management and employee actions when it may be difficult to think ahead due to circumstance.

The following example will demonstrate the importance of policy and compliance to it, and the effects on company profitability of noncompliance:

In a popular local restaurant, complimentary rolls are served to every table. The quality standard for these rolls is that they are to be served golden brown and piping hot. The policy governing how the rolls are to be served states that one roll per guest should be taken to the table at a time.

The guests are free to request more rolls, but on each trip to the table, only one roll per guest should be served. Compliance with this policy ensures that the roll is of the quality it should be, and that the supply of rolls baked by the kitchen remains adequate. Unfortunately, many of the servers find this policy "inconvenient" and will adhere to it only when they feel like doing so, or they will outright ignore it. Some feel that they should serve several rolls because the guest is just going to ask for more anyway, and it will save them a trip to the table. Some worry that the guest will get upset at them for not bringing enough, and will reduce their tip.

Regardless of the reason, the server will bring two or three rolls for each guest. Typically, what happens is that the second roll the guest picks up is just barely warm. The guest eats it, but notices it didn't taste nearly as good as the first. Maybe the first was only so good because they were hungry. After all, they're just rolls. The restaurant is probably just trying to fill you up on bread so you won't notice how small their portions are anyway. By the time the guest picks up the third roll, it has gotten cold. Ugh, that's not tasty at all. Now the guest stops his server to ask for some fresh bread. The server sees that there is still bread on the table and so takes her time to bring more, not realizing that the bread on the table is unwanted. Now the server's original fears are being realized. She brought extra bread so the guest would not get upset and would tip well. The guest wants the bread hot and doesn't understand what is taking the server so long to come back with fresh hot bread. The longer she is away, the more dissatisfied this guest becomes.

This has now happened at several tables in the restaurant, and the amount of wasted bread is growing. A large party, including some small children, have just been seated. They ask their server to bring some extra rolls because the kids will eat them faster than she can bring them. When the server heads to the bread warmer, she finds that it is empty and the timer on the oven still has eight minutes left. The wasted rolls that were just taken out moments before are now costing this second server her tip as well. The new party has irritable children who would be quieted with a roll, allowing the adults to have a pleasant experience.

Even if the server explains that fresh rolls will be coming right out of the oven, the party's first request of the meal was put off and they are dissatisfied already. It's often a downhill experience from there. They look around while waiting for their drinks and rolls, and see that every table around them has rolls. Why don't they have some, too? What's wrong with their server?

Let's look at this from the corporate perspective. Following this bread policy also applies to food cost. Food cost is the cost of any food used, whether it is eaten or thrown away. Food cost takes away from profits. So what does food cost have to do with rolls? Each wasted roll has a cost. In a busy restaurant, thousands of guests are seated each day, meaning thousands of rolls thrown away. The costs add up when looked at over the weeks, months, and the year.

The dissatisfaction of the large party mentioned above is also likely to lead to more costs. They are disappointed from the very start of the meal. The negative tone that has been set is likely to lead to them looking for more things to go wrong. Their food is served, and they don't like how it is cooked. They complain to the server, who gets a manager, who winds up taking the item off their check. This also contributes to food cost. The food left the kitchen and went to the table, so it is used, but the guest doesn't have to pay for the item now, so the food cost increased without increasing profit. Food cost isn't the only concern when guests are dissatisfied. Negative word of mouth advertising is also likely to follow. Each guest in that large party will go and tell their friends and family about what an awful experience they had. They will recommend to the people they know not to waste their time going to such an awful place. This leads to an exponential loss of guests, and of profit.

You can see how what appears to be a simple policy that is just in the way and can be laid aside, is actually very vital to your business. Following a policy, that was laid out in a planning session allows you to keep your business running efficiently during times of action, when the small details can seem unimportant and easy to ignore.

Competence dictates that an excellent manager must be able to get employees to understand the need to follow policy or the company will eventually cease to make a profit. Their future employment can be derailed by something as simple as serving one too many pieces of bread.

If bread seems too mundane to worry about, replace the word bread with bullets, make the restaurant a war zone, and have the employees be soldiers firing indiscriminately, using all their ammunition days before a major attack. Does adhering to policy seem trivial now?

The Influence on My Leadership Style

From my experience in Germany, I learned that modeling the behavior of my supervisor was actually the first step toward developing a leadership style. The Leadership Style Inventory emphasizes four leadership styles. The first style identified by the Leadership Style Inventory is Commanding, a style that focuses on performance, which is the stereotypical view of military leaders. The second LSI style, Logical, pertains to leaders who cover all alternatives. These leaders have long-term goals, use analysis and questioning, and learn by reasoning things through. The Inspirational style is characteristic of those who are able to develop meaningful visions of the future by focusing on radically new ideas; they learn by experimentation. Finally, a Consensus type emphasizes openness and facilitation in the work environment.

Over the course of my twenty years in the military, I found the style that provided the most effective approach depended on the situation; however, the one I chose most often was the participative style of leadership. This style uses problem solving and the decision making input of the employee, allowing them to take ownership of their growth with proper supervision. I had finally learned that I could trust my supervisors to consider my best interests, and that I should seek the advice of a role model when faced with tough decisions. I also learned that to be a good leader myself, I would have to be flexible, resilient, and supportive of my subordinates, not just a figurehead.

Final Leadership Thoughts: 9/11 Strategies of Survival

Leadership is a person's ability to effectively influence a followers' behavior in order to accomplish the job assigned, while looking out for the needs of the organization and the welfare of the people working in it. According to Yukl (2006), leadership is the process of influencing others to understand and agree about what needs to be done and the method of how to accomplish it; the process of facilitating individual and collective efforts to accomplish shared objectives. As I reflect on the various definitions of leadership I have examined over the past eight weeks, leadership development begins with me personally taking an active role as a change agent in my career and finding a simplistic business model to achieve my goals. As a leader and future online educator it is important for me to identify the most effective leadership approach, examine its strengths and weaknesses, create a strategic plan for the future, and facilitate meeting the challenges of virtual learning.

Leadership approaches and models date back to the 1800's with McClelland's Theory of Needs, which studied the dominant innate need of human motivation through the use of the Thematic Apperception Test (McCelland, 1965). Researchers and theorists continued through the present day, studying various approaches to leadership. Behavioral, contingency, transactional, transformational and servant leadership are among some of the most extensively researched methods.

My chosen personal leadership approaches are the behavioral and transformational leadership methods. The behavioral approach, which was popular from mid 1940 to the 1950's, centers on the idea that leaders are made and not born. The focus is on the leader's actions, which can be learned with the proper guidance and teaching. This model focuses on what a leader does and how the leader engages in what he does. I believe behavior is observable and since behavior is observable, you can teach a person how to modify behavior to build relationships, develop employees, and accomplish objectives.

A transformational and charismatic leader is a visionary for leading change in a global society. Transformational leadership is a process that changes and transforms individuals (Northhouse, 2001). I have learned, through a course in Transformational Leadership and Innovation, that transformational leadership emphasizes the study of the bond between a charismatic leader and follower.

In 2005, I started a small business called Customized Global Learning, LLC (CGL, LLC) with the vision of providing global access to education and leadership to clients in businesses, nonprofit organizations, and educational institutions. In 2005, I was unaware that the mission of the CGL, LLC was patterned after the transformational model. This bond is formed through a charismatic approach where the inspired and divine gift captures the imagination of followers (Nahavandi, 1992). Bass (1993) identified the typical behavior of a transformational leader to include: Idealized Influence, Inspiration Motivation, Intellectual Stimulation, and Individual Consideration; this is the type of leadership I want to practice.

Leaders with idealized influence are those whose high ethics and moral conduct influence followers to hold them in high regard. My core values from this principle consist of ethics, honesty, trust, respect, and balanced power. Ethically, I will never intentionally compromise my integrity to gain position, power, or prestige. I will not manipulate colleagues or clients to gain their business or their trust.

If trust is not established there is no effective personal or professional relationship; therefore, I build environments of mutual collaboration and participation. Loyalty is earned through trust, and is not a given right to a person based on position. Respect is to do unto others as you want others to treat you and I will not intentionally disrespect a person or their property. J.R. French and B.H. Raven cites five types of power: legitimate, expert, coercive, referent, and reward (Salzwedel, 2002). Balanced power is a taxonomy of five powers consist of legitimate power (legal influence), expert (knowledge), coercive (punishment), referent (charismatic and earned affirmation) and reward (return on investment or award) used through my leadership skills in accordance to the situation presented. I use this balanced power. Critics of transformational leadership have pointed to the potential for leaders to use their manipulative power in an unethical or self-centered way (Bentley, 2002; DeRuyver, 2001). My definition of balanced power is the overall effective ability of a leader to influence a follower in a moral, legal, and ethical way.

The inspirational motivation of transformational leadership provides followers with challenges and meaning for engaging in shared goals and undertakings (Bass & Steidlmeier, 1999). I envision leadership that builds confidence, stimulates enthusiasm and puts together a strategy for followers who will work within my organization not only based what the organization can do for them, but based on what we, the team, can do for each other.

The intellectual stimulation of transformational leadership incorporates situation evaluation, vision formulation, and patterns of implementation. Such openness has a transcendent, spiritual dimension and helps followers critically analyze assumptions and generate more creative solutions to problems (Bass & Steidlmeir, 1999). As a leader, I believe that the best way to stimulate continual growth in the organization is to challenge the status quo, encouraging followers to become innovative and out-of-the-box thinkers.

Individual consideration is the transformational leader's creative ability to determine a given follower's unique career and professional development. Leaders provide coaching, mentoring, and consulting to followers to encourage growth and development. One of the challenging aspects of my vision is the ability to provide an online learning forum for disadvantaged youth, with adequate funding, resources, and qualified staff. As a transformational leader, I will work to build business and professional partnerships able to assist financially and provide internships. The key to building relationships with others begins with understanding the strengths and weaknesses of my leadership style and using them appropriately.

An empowering experience while attending a course in Transformational Leadership and Innovation, was undertaking a Theory X and Y leadership assessment. Theory X assumes people are naturally lazy and if given the opportunity not to work, they would not work. My style is primarily Theory Y, because I believe the average human being learns, under proper circumstances, to not only accept but also seek responsibility (Wren, 2004). However, with a tendency to want to control and shape my environment, as revealed by the results of my DISC Behavioral Profile, I have a tendency to display characteristics of a Theory X leader. The DISC Profile is based on the work of William Moulton Martson, PhD (1893-1947) who examined behavior of individuals in a specific situation within their environment. The four-quadrant model created from his work reveals that a person's behavior falls in the dimensions of dominance, inspiration, steadiness, or conscientiousness, while identifying their strengths and weaknesses.

My strength is based on shaping the environment for key leaders and followers to perform well; allowing creativity, and moving barriers to accomplishing their subtasks are part of my responsibility. Ten characteristics of my strengths, as revealed by my DISC profile, included authority, self-promotion, emotionalism, low egocentricity, trust, good communication skills, problem solving, generosity, competence, and influence.

Authority: I approach a leadership situation to solve problems and overcome obstacles and get the job accomplished. I work best when given a difficult situation to solve or upon receipt of a receiving the shock to my personal worldview. Although I like some control over my environment, I get a much greater satisfaction from employees solving and overcoming problems through my coaching or working collaboratively with their colleagues and employees.

Self-promotion: Informing others about me and offering my expertise and experience to others is a natural extension of my personality. This is strength, when forged together with others. Self-promotion is a weakness when overused or not managed properly. The impression that I am conceited will then be felt amongst ones team or colleagues.

Emotionalism: I cannot recall how many times I was reminded in my twenty-one years of military service to be careful not to sound emotional, even though emotions are a natural part of a leader's behavior. Given a situation with a unclear or easy identifiable solution, I will tend make a decision based on what I feel is the right thing to do and I am willing to openly talk about the situation with the person for resolution. Overwhelmingly, overused emotion when speaking to others candidly can sometimes make others feel angry or uncomfortable.

Egocentricity: Chaos, unexpected events, and great opposition do not arbitrarily hinder me from accomplishing goals. Being self-focused is strength when it benefits the person or team. Self-focus can help team members and myself accomplish our goals when team members become unfocused. The weakness of egocentricity is too much introspection gives the impression that I am self-absorbed.

Trust: The tendency to believe in what a person says or does without validating their position is a trait I embrace, unless proven otherwise. Noble as trust may seem, overused trust is naïve leadership and can lead to mistrust when positions are not validated.

Communication: The ability to adequately communicate one's message through written or oral mediums, providing feedback, modeling and good listening skills are strengths in my leadership style.

According to Goffer (2004), effective leaders are good communicators, while skillful leaders ensure that they use the right mode of communication for the situation and person. Effective communicators are able to build a bridge that transmits the behavioral intent of the organization to followers, creating the foundation for trust. Levering

(1998) cites that communication has long been shown to be a critical factor in superior worker motivation and performance and has great potential to aid organizations in their quest for committed workers. Overusing communication skills by talking too much results in people tuning you out, meaning they might miss vital information. Overused communication can rambling orally, as well as, in writing. Additionally, clear-cut communication can sound rude, thus alienating the communicator from colleagues.

Proficient: My twenty-one years of military leadership qualify me as an expert in military leadership and provide me with technical knowledge of communication skills. Bass & Aviolo, (1993) claim that competence is the universal expectation that a person is able to get things done for the business unit with a winning record of accomplishment. This is a sign of expert knowledge. My weakness stems in translating military experience into civilian experience. Education in leadership and business perspective required that I attend a formal program.

Problem Solving and Decision Making: Identifying the real problem within the context of the situation is the first step of resolving an issue. The challenge is that the real issue may be masked by other issues, such as lateness, low morale, or theft by a government leader. The seven-step process that I use was adapted from military service: identify the problem, gather information, develop a course of action, analyze and compare courses of action, make a decision, make a plan, and implement a plan. My strength lies in the ability to have a keen intuition of the underlying issue in the context of the problem. My weakness is making a hasty decision without validating the results.

Generosity: Sharing knowledge, resources and my time is something I am liberal about with clients and colleagues, never expecting a return on investment on the time spent with them. This trait works favorably in achieving common goals. The weakness is remembering to say no to clients and colleagues when my scheduled is overloaded.

Influence: Inspiring others to move to action is a trait of an effective leader. Acting as a mentor or advocate to others when they cannot advocate for themselves is a trait that I model. However, the weakness of influence lies in making assessments in a considerate tone to encourage self-empowerment without sounding manipulative or harsh, which defeats the original intent of the influence.

Conclusion: November 2008

Some people read the conclusion to determine if they will want to read the book. Here I am going to break the mode of the traditional conclusion by providing a brief "Take Away Thought". In life we experience different seasons. The times when things are working well: good job, content marriage, decent health, and happy children Now in reality, this may be a short season in many people lives. The truth is that in this life things are constantly changing, and so are people and the environment they must work and live. September 11, the Katrina incident or similar events may not provide a template for us to work or live by. Yet, if we look deep inside ourselves, we have principles by which we function. I call them strategies of survival for workplace, leadership , and life. My principles of survival are from my entry journals of the Pentagon, September 11th event and from various parts of my career and life. I hope that you will adopt some of these principles and begin to write your own model of survival guidelines by which to work and to live by. In August 2008, I was actually in New Orleans where the Katrina devastation took place. Katrina is going on its three-year anniversary the end of this month and the visible devastation is still extremely prevalent. One area of New Orleans is vibrant, another area is renewed, and still hundreds, if not thousands of homes, are still utterly ruined. This sends chills down my spine, as I reflect on the devastation from 9/11; however, the structure from 9/11 is rebuilt. The project was completed almost in a year. A reminder of renewed strength. May we never forget the challenges that others face and become desensitized to life's unexpected challenges. My final words: When it looks like you have, or may lose you everything important to you, you still have a powerful future ahead of you if you hold onto your Faith. Faith is the one aspect of life, no one can take from you, but with "Faith" your future is greater and brighter. Just watch and see!

REFERENCES

Alessandra, T, PhD, CSP, CPAE (2008). The Platinum Rule Workbook. Alessandra & Associates Inc.

Bass, B. M., & Aviolo, B. (1993). Transformational Leadership: A Response to Critiques. In M. M. Chemers & R. Ayman

Bass, B., & Steidlmeier, P. (1999, Summer). Ethics, Character and Authentic Transformational Leadership Behavior.

Bentley, D. (2002). Naked Leadership. Management Today, November/December, 40.

Burns, J. M. (1978). Leadership. New York: Harper & Row. Can Boeing Reinvent Itself? (1993, March 8). Fortune.

Cooperman, L. (2007). Information Literacy and the School Media Center. 47 (94). Retrieved from Fall 2007, from EBSCOHOST database.

Dau, L. (2004). UM News. *Why am I feeling so stressed?*. Retrieved August 10, 2008, from http://www1.umn.edu/umnnews/Feature Stories/workplace stress.html

DeRuyver, D. (2001). The Role of Ethics in Leadership. Leadership: Emerging Directions, August 1-3.

Duxbury, L., Higgins, C. (1997), "Supportive managers: what are they? Why do they matter?", *HRM Research Quarterly*, Vol. 1 No.4, pp.1-5.

Goffee, R., & Jones, G. (2006, October 26). THIS TIME IT'S PERSONAL. (Cover story). People Management, 12(21), 28-34. Retrieved February 3, 2008, from MasterFILE Premier database.

Goman, C. K. (1991). Managing for Commitment: Developing Loyalty Within Organizations. Menlo Park, CA.: Crisp Publications, Inc.

Graen, George B. and Uhl-Bien, Mary (1995). Relationship-Based Approach to Leadership: Development of Leader-Member Exchange (LMX) Theory of Leadership Over 25 Years: Applying a Multi-Level Multi-Domain Perspective. Leadership Quarterly, Summer, pp 219-247. °1995 by Inscape Publishing, Inc. All rights reserved. "Coping & Stress Profile" is a registered trademark of

Inscape Publishing, Inc. *Coping & Stress Profile® Research Report.*

Kubler-Ross, E. (1969). On Death and Dying. New York: Macmillian.

Levering, R. (1998). A Great Place to Work. NY Avon.

Marston, W. M. (1928) Emotions of Normal People. London Kegan Paul, Trench, Trubner Co. Ltd. New York Harcourt.

Martin, R. (2007, June). How Successful Leaders Think. (cover story). *Harvard Business Review*, 85(6), 60-67. Retrieved February 4, 2008, from Business Source Complete database. Brace And Company. Printed In Great Britain by The Devonshire Press, Torquay.

McClelland, D. C. (1965). N-achievement and Entrepreneurship: A Longitudinal Study. Journal of Personality and Social Psychology, 1, 389–392.

Moss, T. (2008) What is Post Traumatic Stress Disorder? A National Center for PTSD Fact Sheet. National Center for Post-Traumatic Stress Disorder, Department of Veterans Affairs

National Center for Post-Traumatic Stress Disorder, Department of Veterans Affairs: Fact Sheet (n.d.). The United States Department of the Army Veteran Affairs. Retrieved July 10, 2008, from http://www.mentalhealth.va.gov/MENTALHEALTH/ptsd/fs_what_is_ptsd0ddb.asp

Nahavandi, A., Mizzi, P. J.,& Malekzadeh, A. R. (1992). Executive's Type A Personality as a Determinant of Environmental Perception and Firm Strategy. Journal of Social Psychology, 132, 59–68.

NCO Creed (2005). Armystudyguide.com. Retrieved July 10, 2008, from http://www.armystudyguide.com/content/army_board_study_guide_topics/nco_history/nco-creed.shtml

Northouse, P. G. (2001). Leadership Theory and Practice, Second Edition. Thousand Oaks, CA: Sage Publications, Inc.

Reardon K &, Reardon. K. J. (1999). "All That We Can Be:" Leading the U.S. Army's Gender Integration Effort. Management Communication Quarterly : McQ, 12(4), 600-617. Retrieved February 1, 2008, from ABI/INFORM Global Database. (Document ID: 40753095).

Salzwedel, D. (2002, June). Leadership and power. Executive Excellence, 19(6), 5. Retrieved November 26, 2008, from ABI/INFORM Global database. (Document ID: 125045781).

Sayer , J. (2007). A Matter of Character. Vital Speeches of the Day, 73(3), 114-115. Retrieved February 2, 2008, from ABI/INFORM Global database. (Document ID: 1231490311).

Tsadik, R. (2007, March). IBM Knows Mother. Incentive, 181(3), 39-39. Retrieved February 3, 2008, from MasterFILE Premier Database.

Wesley A Scroggins (2008). The Relationship Between Employee Fit Perceptions, Job Performance, and Retention: Implications of Perceived Fit. Employee Responsibilities and Rights Journal, 20(1), 57-71.

Retrieved November 1, 2008, from ABI/INFORM Global database. (Document ID: 1427166171).

Yukl, G. (2006). Leadership in Organizations (6th ed.). Upper Saddle River: Pearson.

About the Author

Author, motivational speaker, and education leadership coach Trina speaks to audiences in various parts of the United States and abroad including Korea, Germany, India, Russia, Kenya, and Uganda. Trina completed 20 years of successful military service fulfilling her goal of an Army First Sergeant.

She has earned a Bachelor's Degree in Social Psychology, a Masters in Education, and pursuing a doctorate in Education and Leadership with Education Technology emphasis. Trina is the founder of a for profit Customized Global Learning, LLC and nonprofit Ceempowerment meeting the educational and leadership needs of the diverse learner. To invite Trina Hines to your next event or learn more about services offered call today (571) 330-4844 or visit www.hinescgl.com or www.ceempowerment.org.

Printed in the United States
140516LV00002B/79/P